Constantin Brancusi

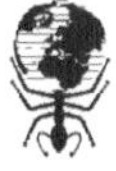

In the same series

Jean Genet Stephen Barber	**Octavio Paz** Nick Caistor
Michel Foucault David Macey	**Walter Benjamin** Esther Leslie
Pablo Picasso Mary Ann Caws	**Charles Baudelaire** Rosemary Lloyd
Franz Kafka Sander L. Gilman	**Jean Cocteau** James S. Williams
Guy Debord Andy Merrifield	**Sergei Eisenstein** Mike O'Mahony
Marcel Duchamp Caroline Cros	**Salvador Dalí** Mary Ann Caws
James Joyce Andrew Gibson	**Edgar Allan Poe** Kevin J. Hayes
Frank Lloyd Wright Robert McCarter	**Gertrude Stein** Lucy Daniel
Jean-Paul Sartre Andrew Leak	**Samuel Beckett** Andrew Gibson
Noam Chomsky Wolfgang B. Sperlich	**Pablo Neruda** Dominic Moran
Jorge Luis Borges Jason Wilson	**William S. Burroughs** Phil Baker
Erik Satie Mary E. Davis	**Stéphane Mallarmé** Roger Pearson
Georges Bataille Stuart Kendall	**Vladimir Nabokov** Barbara Wyllie
Ludwig Wittgenstein Edward Kanterian	

Constantin Brancusi

Sanda Miller

REAKTION BOOKS

To Giulia

Published by Reaktion Books Ltd
33 Great Sutton Street
London EC1V 0DX, UK

www.reaktionbooks.co.uk

First published 2010
Transferred to digital printing 2012

Publication of this book is supported by Southampton Solent University
Art and Design Capability Fund.

Printed and bound by CPI Group (UK) Ltd, Croydon, CR0 4YY

British Library Cataloguing in Publication Data

Miller, Sanda
    Constantin Brancusi. — (Critical lives)
    1. Brancusi, Constantin, 1876-1957. 2. Sculptors,
Romania—Biography.
    I. Title II. Series
    730.9'2-DC22

ISBN 978 1 86189 652 0

Contents

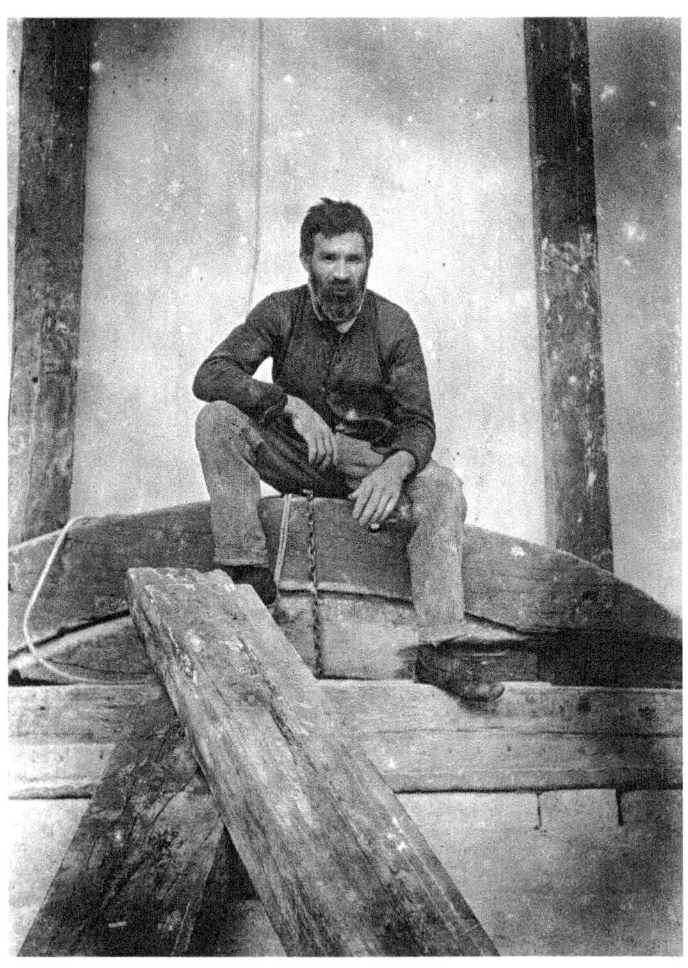

Brancusi in his studio, *c.* 1915.

Introduction

Although Constantin Brancusi is acknowledged as a major artist of the twentieth century, he continues to be one of its most elusive. Two reasons for this spring to mind. The first is to do with his personal history. Brancusi was born and grew up in Romania during the last quarter of the nineteenth century, and despite the West's modernizing influences, Romania was then an impoverished, largely rural land, one regarded by outsiders as a grim Balkan backwater haunted by vampires and werewolves. The second, and to my mind more interesting, reason is that Brancusi himself, once he was settled in Paris, capitalized on the widespread ignorance and prejudices concerning Romania and its inhabitants. Quick to realize that fiction is more appealing to the popular imagination than are facts, he wove around himself a veritable aura of 'otherness' in his celebrated white *atelier* or studio in the heart of Montparnasse. So successful was he in this that we even have a novelistic biography of Brancusi by Peter Neagoe entitled *The Saint of Montparnasse*, published five years after the author's death in 1960, and which was written in order to enshrine the myth forever.[1]

Documentary evidence, however, has continued to emerge, some as recently as 2003,[2] which contradicts such one-dimensional hagiographies, and a more complex picture is emerging, one that reveals Brancusi as a man of his time who responded to the challenge of one of the most turbulent periods in European history, dominated by two world wars and a holocaust, by creating works of haunting and unforgettable beauty.

Brancusi's *oeuvre* is displayed in the foremost museums of Europe and the USA and some of his sculptures, such as the famous *Mlle Pogany*, have achieved iconic status. Less well known is his reconstructed studio complex in Paris, part of the Beaubourg district's Centre Pompidou. A veritable *Gesamtkunstwerk* that encapsulates Brancusi's life and work, the 'Atelier Brancusi' is his most enduring legacy. In his lifetime in Montparnasse it was the stage on which his carefully construed 'otherness' was played out to a captive audience. This audience comprised the dealers, collectors, friends, lovers, writers, critics and the odd sycophantic hanger-on that Brancusi had gathered around him. Some who visited have left precious testimonies, as the following example reveals. During the 1950s the playwright Eugène Ionesco was invited to visit Brancusi. Although 'le pittoresque da sa personne' – as Ionesco sarcastically put it – did not appeal to him, one cold winter evening he did accept the invitation. As he was waiting by the stove in the company of the painter Alexandre Istrati, the door opened and in stepped Brancusi, 'a little old man about 80 years old, cudgel in hand, wearing a tall white furry bonnet on his head; a patriarch's white beard' and 'les yeux pétillants de malice'. Although informed of his visitor's identity, Brancusi feigned ignorance by asking Ionesco 'what was his *métier*'. Istrati explained that Ionescu 'is a playwright, writes for the stage'. Brancusi replied 'Me, I detest the theatre, I have no need of theatre. *J'emmerde le théâtre*.' But in Ionesco he found his equal, for Ionesco quickly retorted that 'I too detest and *J'emmerde* it. That is the reason I write plays to mock it. It is the sole reason.' Brancusi, who was famed for provoking his interlocutors by playing devil's advocate, then began a rambling peroration about Hitler being a misunderstood hero, about Aryanism, then in turn his hatred of Nazism, his hatred of democracy, of bolshevism, of anti-communism, of science, of modernism, of anti-modernism and so on . . . . But Ionesco kept very, very quiet. Defeated, Brancusi left the room, only to reappear moments later carrying a bottle of champagne.[3]

Brancusi's disdain for critics was legendary. Thus in 1921 he turned down Ezra Pound's offer (Pound was then the editor of *The Little Review*) to write a book about him.[4] There were, however, exceptions, especially if they happened to be young and attractive females, such as the journalist Jeanne Robert Foster, who in 1922 published an article on Brancusi in *Vanity Fair*. Notwithstanding the rather backhanded compliment of calling him 'an elderly faun' (he was not yet 50 years of age), she described him as 'a singularly handsome man, of great personal distinction, broad-shouldered, with a noble head covered with curly black hair. His black beard streaked with white, the lightness of his movements, the dancing light in his eyes, gave him the look of an elderly faun.'[5]

Brancusi's general resistance to publications devoted to him also explains why no books on him were published in French during his lifetime, with the little-known exception of one in 1947 by Brancusi's friend from Romania, V. G. Paleolog. Since Paleolog had both to both finance and publish it, only 375 copies were printed.[6] Although Paleolog had known Brancusi since 1910,[7] only a rather bizarre reference regarding Brancusi's background can be found in the book:

Descended from the peasant nobility, ethnically the best preserved from heterogeneous contacts . . . Brancusi leaves us an *oeuvre* which is difficult to incorporate within the mainstream of Romanian art, with the exception of two significant works: *The Prayer* and *the Wisdom of the Earth*.[8]

An interesting reference to Brancusi's sculptures, at the time when he was little known outside avant-garde circles, is that by the aristocratic Romanian poetess and Parisian socialite Marie Bengesco. She contributed a chapter on culture entitled 'L'Art en Roumanie' in a book on Romania published in Paris in 1919, *La Roumanie en images*. In it she provided an astute aperçu regarding our subject's artistic progress: 'Brancusi, who affirmed himself initially as a powerful realist, now rejects the modern techniques which seem to him to have fulfilled their scope and tries to say new things in a primitive art.'[9]

Brancusi's reluctance to allow his friends to write about him, or to furnish them with photographs of his works he himself took after being taught the rudiments of photography by Man Ray, explains why only one monograph was published on him immediately after his death in 1957, by the English architect David Lewis.[10]

The editor of the *Cahiers d'art*, Christian Zervos, however, published during the same year a touching homage dedicated to Brancusi. The list of contributors – which included Jean Arp, Giulio Carlo Argan, Carola Giedion-Welcker, Peggy Guggenheim, Herbert Read, John Rothenstein and J. J. Sweeney – is the most enduring testimony of the admiration accorded Brancusi by the international art community.[11] It is also worth mentioning the obituary written by Herbert Read for *The Listener*, which attracted an acrimonious response by Douglas Cooper, who accused Read of inaccuracies. Read regarded Brancusi's sculpture as far from perfect, especially in instances such as *Mlle Pogany*, which disturbed him because of its

> quality of utter sophistication, of utter refinement rather than utter simplicity. . . . There are several versions of 'Mademoiselle Pogany', spaced from 1913 to 1931, and they show a progressive elimination of the sophisticated elements I refer to, but even in the final version I am still disturbed by a slick suavity wholly absent from his greatest works.[12]

In 1959 Carola Giedion-Welcker's monograph on Brancusi was published,[13] followed in 1963 by Ionel Jianou's book in French and English editions.[14] At that point Jianou calculated that there had been 'seven books and more than three hundred studies, chronicles, homages, exhibitions and testimonies on Brancusi, who is at present regarded as one of the most influential artists of the twentieth century'.[15]

For much of his life Brancusi was in the habit of jotting down
his thoughts on random pieces of paper, some of which had been
published here and there, but it was not until the catalogue of
the exhibition *La Dation Brancusi 2001 (Dessins et archives)* was
published in 2003 that the full extent was known. The chapter
entitled 'Brancusi: Le Jeu de l'écrit' contains more than two hundred
such *notes manuscrites* discovered in Brancusi's handwriting.[16] One
such, dated to about 1919, is rendered even more poignant by
Brancusi's terrible French:

> *Je pleur – il fait telman beau dans mon âme, mon Coeur se dechire*
> *persone au tour de moi – persone.*[17]

> I cry – it is so beautiful in my soul, my Heart tears itself apart
> nobody around me – nobody.

But this is only one part of the picture; the flip side presents another:
a gregarious and generous person who loved to entertain, eat, drink,
make merry, make love . . . pursuits undertaken on a heroic scale.
Testament to this is not only the voluminous private correspondence
between Brancusi and his friends, lovers, dealers and collectors, which
was only recently made available, but also the humorous and affectionate accounts of those bucolic feasts that unravelled in the intimacy
of the white studio.

Of course, the most precious testimonies are Brancusi's sculptures:
the silent legacy that – as Brancusi himself said – could only be unlocked
if you look at them from the heart: 'Regardez-les jusqu-à ce que vous
les voyiez. Les plus près de Dieu les on vues.'

1

Childhood

Brancusi's inauspicious birth on 21 February 1876[1] took place in a tiny village in western Wallachia of the sort that was typical of rural Romania in the later nineteenth century: Hobiţa was humble and its inhabitants were poor. Romania was primarily a country of farms and forests, and as a consequence, 'large gardens with adjacent stables and sometimes even extensive fields separate one house from another, so that villages with houses set close to each other . . . do not exist'. As for house interiors, these were 'everywhere very simple'. In the summer months country people spent the nights under the sky, either sleeping in fields in order to be near their herds or flocks or on a *prispa* (a roofed and balustraded open loggia attached to the house), using the interior of the house more as a shelter for the winter months or during bad weather.[2]

As a rule the two points of focus that dominated village life were the church and its cemetery. Regarded as the collective responsibility of the community, no efforts were spared to provide the village with a worthy monument in which to worship:

Each village will take pride in making the divine abode worthy of the house of the Saviour. The impoverished artist will carve the beams of the roof and the stalls lining the walls, he will get an artisan of his class to paint the frescoes that display their colours on the walls, both inside and out, to carve the stone frames of the doors and windows, to carve and gild the iconostasis, a marvel of

lightness of proportion and technique that divides the church
into two parts, one set apart for the priest and called the altar,
the other more spacious for the congregation.[3]

The cemetery was a sombre place whose crosses, projected against the
cloudless blue sky, 'were reminiscent of Golgotha'.[4] But the houses
were nonetheless of special significance in the life of the village as
they presented an altogether different kind of challenge because of
the meagre material means available: 'In every house with its white
walls glistening in the sun, there is little furniture, nothing beyond
the essentials of a humble life, all labour and self-denial'.[5]

Further confirmation of this sorry state of affairs comes from
numerous accounts left by travellers. In 1879 in his *Lettres du Bosphore:
Bucharest, Constantinopole, Athènes,* the aristocrat and French diplo-
mat Charles de Moüy gave a depressing account of Brancusi's native
region of Oltenia, whose houses looked like 'haystacks': 'man, house
and field blend in a uniform block, bound to each other, suffering
the same fate, having the same dark and sombre look'. What he
encountered in Oltenia he regarded as nothing more or less than
'a corner of society in the Orient, sombre and picturesque, miserable
and rich in colour'. The River Olt itself struck him as being 'a solitary
presence in the middle of limitless space'.[6]

It is the more remarkable then that no efforts were spared
by Romanians to render the humblest abode as visually attractive
as possible. The priorities of the rural working class had to be
pragmatic rather than aesthetic, and for that reason the typical
household was in fact like an extended family since it involved the
(absolutely vital) livestock too: 'In front there is usually a large yard
full of life and swarming with animals and birds, the cart, the sleigh
which takes its place in winter, the plough, the firewood, the hay
for the animals . . . '.[7] Yet the pride and joy of each household was
its entrance gate, whose ornament and beauty were considered
without parallel in Europe.[8]

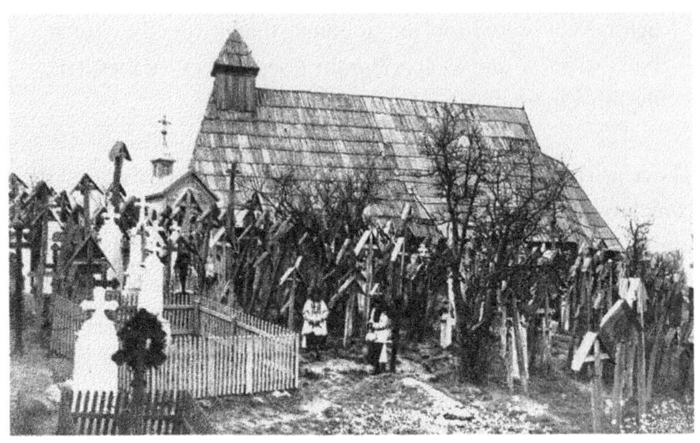

A church and cemetery in Gorj county, Oltenia, in the late 19th century.

Brancusi grew up in just such a house of modest pretensions, fortunately now preserved with minimal alteration as a museum.[9] It consists of two rooms separated by a living space containing the *laviţa* (stove) that doubled as a kitchen. The exterior, with its whitewashed walls, is dominated by the *prispa* that props up a pitched shingle roof. Inside, the rooms are filled with coloured textiles and lovingly decorated furniture and utensils. Every object down to the humblest cup or spoon is decorated, incised, carved or painted. The floor, furniture and walls are covered with carpets, towels, tablecloths and bedspreads as well as the ubiquitous icons. This was the environment that surrounded Brancusi from the moment of his birth and both constituted his first visual stimuli and (as repeatedly pointed out in subsequent works[10]) the earliest source of inspiration for the morphology of his sculptures.

Even after years of living in Paris, where he became thoroughly entrenched in its avant-garde culture, his modest background and perhaps a somewhat affected 'otherness' continued to prevail, as Paul Morand perceptively commented in the catalogue text for Brancusi's one-man show held in 1926 at the Brummer Gallery in New York:

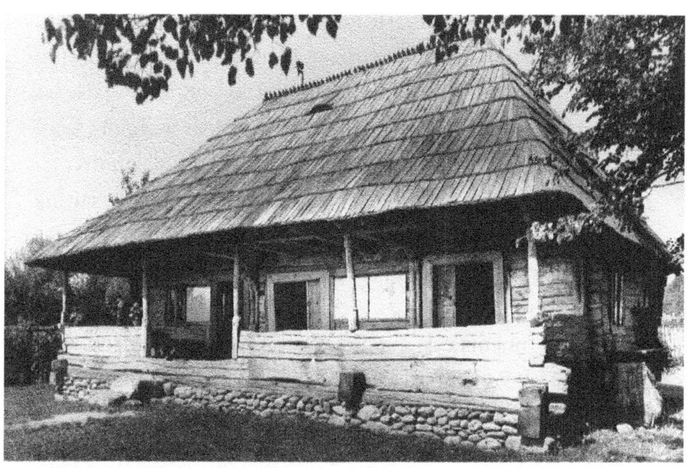

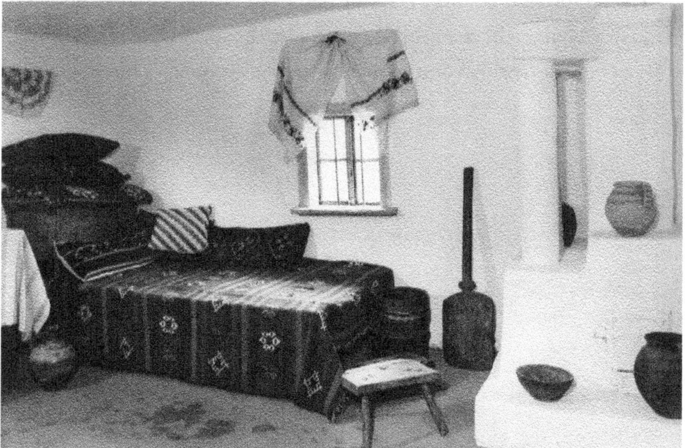

Brancusi's house in Hobiţa, Gorj county, in the region of Oltenia, south-west Romania. Built by his father, *c.* 1870, Brancusi's sister Fîrsina Brânză inherited it. She had the house removed from its original location and set up on a new foundation 200 metres away. This rebuilt home is now the Brancusi museum.

The interior of Brancusi's house, A typical 19th-century Romanian peasant interior.

Brancusi is a born artisan. He knows nothing of pupils, assistants, stone-pointers, polishers or cutters. He does everything for himself. His materials are always true to him, always faithful. He has approached them from every angle. Brancusi, as we know, is a Romanian of the old peasant stock of that beautiful country. . . . He works on without masters nor disciples, without advertising, without toadying art critics. The extreme freedom of Paris has allowed Brancusi to remain the least 'Parisian' of Romanians.[11]

Brancusi's Romania was not only vastly different from sophisticated *fin-de-siècle* Paris, it was also very unlike the state that became modern Romania on acquiring its present boundaries at the Treaty of Trianon following Europe's cataclysmic Great War of 1914–18.[12]

The region of the Lower Danube had been invaded and reduced to Turkish vassalage in the mid-fifteenth century, and was technically still part of the Turkish empire at the time of Brancusi's birth. Only

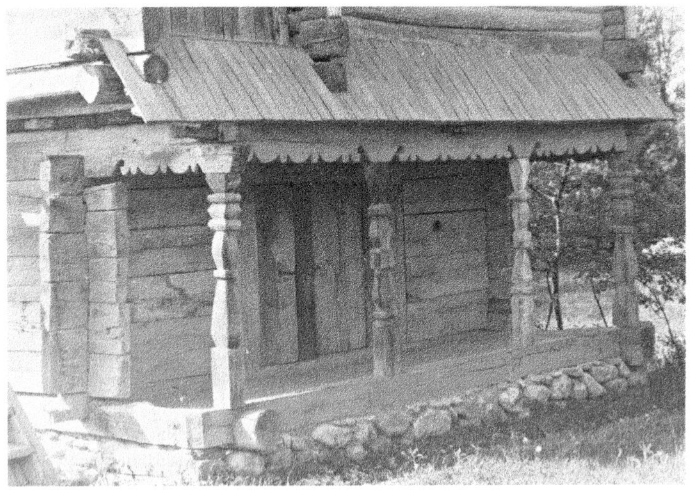

The Romanian open loggia or *prispa* provided unlimited scope for the display of wood-carving. Supporting pillars often carry motifs that can be discerned in Brancusi's work.

with the Treaty of Paris in 1856 had Moldavia and Wallachia been guaranteed protection as principalities with identical administrative systems (Transylvania and Banat continued as part of the Austro-Hungarian empire until 1920); six years later the two principalities combined, adopting the name Romania. Full independence from Turkey followed in 1877, and four years later Prince Carol de Hohenzollern-Singmaringen was elevated to King Carol i; he ruled the country until his death in 1914.

The end of serfdom had come late in this part of the world – in 1746 in Wallachia and 1749 in Moldavia. A century later, Alexandru Ioan Cuza (1820–1873), regarded as the founder of modern Romania, ruled the United Principalities of Moldavia and Wallachia from 1859 to 1866. In a brave attempt to emancipate the rural working class he passed a law whereby peasants were allowed to own their allotments. Unfortunately his good intentions backfired, for landowners regarded themselves as under no obligation to allow peasants to live and work on allotments that remained in gentry ownership. As a consequence the peasants were forced to sell their labour cheaply in order to survive, and a third class – that of the middle-men – emerged, whose sole justification to exist was to negotiate between landowners and peasants by contracting the latter to work for the former. The tension generated by this deteriorating state of affairs culminated in 1907 with one of the bloodiest uprisings in Romanian history, during which tens of thousands of peasants were massacred.[13]

Fortunately, life in Hobiţa during Brâncusi's childhood was peaceful, following the secular patterns of ancient rural communities at a time when transhumance was still practiced. It shaped Brancusi's earliest memories and developed his love of nature with its wealth of birds and animals, which he later captured with such deep understanding in his sculptures. Thus Brancusi's formative years were shielded from much of the turmoil Romania was undergoing elsewhere during the painful process of emancipation that turned a medieval backwater into a Westernizing capitalist state in less than fifty years.

Brancusi was the fourth child of Nicolae Brâncuşi (1832–1884),
who (according to an ancient Romanian custom) subsequently
changed his first name to Radu, and his wife Maria Deaconescu,
a spinner by trade. They had married in 1872; the bridegroom was
then forty years of age and the bride twenty-one. It was the groom's
second marriage, for Nicolae was previously married to a woman
named Ilinca, with whom he had three children, Ion (nicknamed
Chijnea), Vasile and Gheorghe, before her early death. With Maria,
Nicolae went on to father four more – Grigore, Constantin, Dumitru
and Eufrosina – but by the time of the birth of his daughter Eufrosina
in 1884 he was dead too, leaving his young wife to bring up seven
children. Maria lived on into her late sixties, dying in 1919.[14]

Brancusi's childhood was brief, and the little we glean from
existing accounts tell us it was not a happy one. He was deprived
of an elementary school education at Hobiţa and by the age of seven,
a short time before his father's death, Brancusi, as remembered by
a childhood friend, was a working lad,

> first looking after his parents' cattle and later [employed] as a
> shepherd in a Carpathian sheepfold. This involved a tough
> apprenticeship, and enabled him to acquaint himself with the
> life of nature, with the secrets of the plants, the movements of
> the stars which announced the dawn, the meaning of the clouds
> which foretold the coming of rain, storm or fine weather. . . .
> His schooling was far harsher and far more useful than the usual
> sort: His teachers were Life and Nature. During the hard winters,
> he liked to model forms invented by his rich and childlike imagi-
> nation in the sparkling crystals of the heavy snow. These delighted
> the village children and impressed the peasants, for they evoked a
> world of invisible powers. Brancusi later admitted that the image
> of these sculptures in frozen snow, made when he was a child,
> haunted him for the rest of his life.[15]

Nevertheless, he was proud of his origins and family, and later recalled with pride that his father was *un om umblat* ('a travelled man'). This peripatetic parent

> had been to Craiova, he even reached Bucharest. In the village, houses had small holes covered with paper for windows. When he returned from his journeying, he introduced an innovation: he enlarged the windows [of his house] and made them open. Everybody else followed suit. Today all the houses are beautiful with large windows.[16]

What little schooling Brancusi did receive took place in the neighbouring villages of Peştişani and Brediceni, as his former schoolmate Vasile Blendea recalled:

> We started school together in Peştişani . . . he remained there for two years. The teacher's name was Zaharia. Once he scratched something on his desk with his pocket knife and the teacher punished him by locking him up in a dirty cupboard. He ran away and never came back. He started in Brediceni where the teacher was Petre Brancusi and there he finished the remaining years of his primary school. I did not finish mine. He was clever, understood quickly and liked to know everything.[17]

The most unequivocal statement Brancusi himself made about his childhood is that he repeatedly attempted to run away from home: this happened twice, in 1887 and 1888, and there may have been a third attempt; he was then not yet twelve years of age.[18] His life as a small boy was bleakly curtailed by the harsh realities of life, and apart from the handful of accounts already referred to – whose reliability could be argued to verge on the apocryphal – we are ignorant about his upbringing. Nor do we have any material testimonies he might have wrought and left behind in the Romanian world of his childhood, with one possible exception: Brancusi is alleged to have decorated seven wooden pillars of the loggia of a house belonging to the priest of the neighbouring village of Romanesti. This is claimed to have happened during a visit in 1896–8, when Brancusi was already a pupil at the School of Arts and Crafts in Craiova.[19] What is important, however, is that these early years spent in Hobiţa and neighbouring villages constitute Brancusi's earliest artistic stimuli, out of which he started to shape a possible career.

2

Craiova and Apprenticeship

In 1888, aged 12, Brancusi left Hobiţa to find work in Craiova, a provincial capital in Dolj county about 100 kilometres south of Hobiţa, where he would spend the following ten years, initially working crushingly long hours in cafés and restaurants washing glasses and dishes or waiting on tables. For a country boy, Craiova must have appeared awesome. Back in 1846 a woman traveller had declared it to be a 'superb town, regularly built, with bridges, a bazaar covered with a roof made of wooden planks' and 'about 80,000 inhabitants'.[1] In the 1880s the town was undergoing a process of Westernization that was particularly noticeable in the intense programme of architectural development that provided Brancusi's first intimations of the other Europe lying further west.[2] But the modernizing ethos did not affect sculpture and painting at the same time as it did architecture in Romania, and anyway Craiova lagged behind to some extent. It has been supposed that Brancusi's first experiences of sculpture must in fact have been the *fin-de-siècle* traditional funerary monuments he would have encountered locally, for in Craiova in those days,

apart from the wayside crosses of the fountains situated at the outskirts of the town, not even a single public monument existed. To strengthen his concept of sculpture, the pupil Brancusi had to wander through the cemetery, where among the wooden or stone funerary crosses, here and there was something that could be called a bust or a statue.[3]

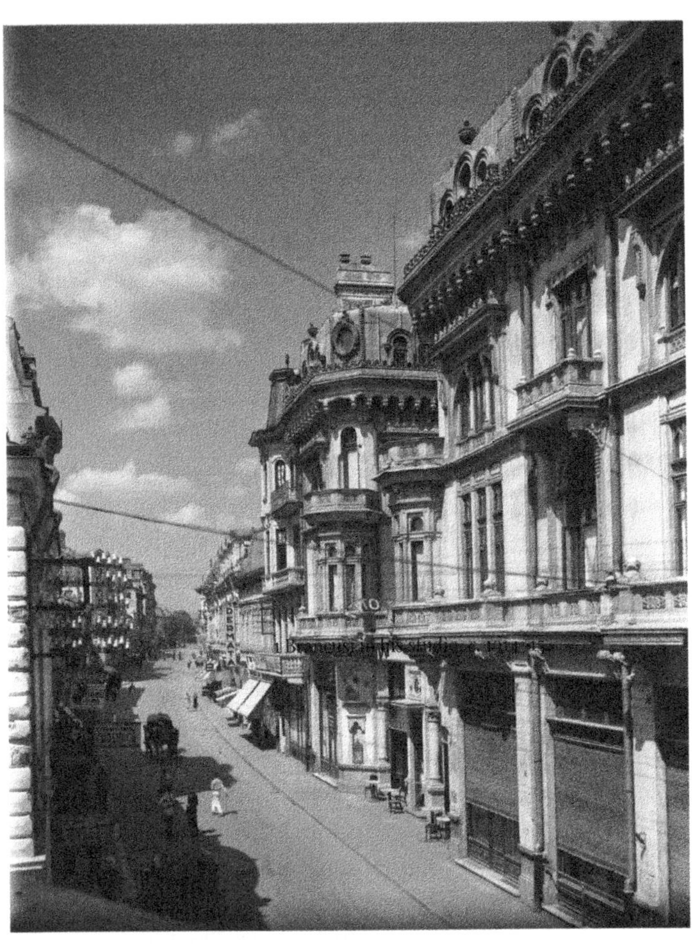

Unirii Street in Craiova in 1898, illustrating the Western European influence on the architecture of a provincial city in the newly independent Romanian state.

The foundation in 1865 of the Faculty of Sculpture at the Academy
of Fine Arts in Bucharest marked the beginning of the emergence
of a modern Romanian school of sculpture, whose influence later
impacted on Craiova. Nevertheless, two of the pioneers of Romanian
modern sculpture, Giorgio Vasilescu (1864–1898)[4] and Constantin
Bălăcescu (1865–1913),[5] were both trained at the School of Arts and
Crafts in Craiova before leaving for Italy to continue their academic
studies.[6] It is not known whether Brancusi met either of these
sculptors, both of whom were living in Craiova when he arrived in
1894. The former became known to a larger world by means of a
public monument commissioned by the neighbouring town of Ploeşti,
completed in 1896, a work that Brancusi may well have heard of, and
possibly even went to see. More certain is that he would have seen
Bălăcescu's public monument dedicated to the Romanian national
hero Tudor Vladimirescu erected in Tîrgu-Jiu and inaugurated in 1898,
an important event that would not have escaped the young Brancusi.[7]

But the type of work still dominating Bălăcescu's professional
career in Romania was funerary sculpture, which was popular
with the emerging Romanian bourgeoisie who wanted to emulate
Western European fashions. Like most other sculptors, Bălăcescu
made a living from these commissions and was therefore obliged
to comply with conservative Romanian taste, which favoured a
retardataire neo-classical style redolent of allegorical figures in
distress accompanied by angels and an assortment of heraldic
animals and birds. He received numerous commissions, and his
work can be found in the cemeteries of Bucharest, Craiova, Tîrgu-Jiu,
Caracal and elsewhere. Despite the often excessive ornamentation
(allegorical figures, angels, crosses, eagles and so on) these funereal
monuments are above other examples within the same genre that
were 'imported from abroad in industrial quantities'.[8]

In the late nineteenth century Craiova was undergoing an
intense period of artistic activity, with artists working mostly on
commission for a well-heeled bourgeoisie while teaching subjects

such as calligraphy and drawing in its *lycées* to supplement their incomes. One of the most outstanding painters contemporary with Brancusi was Francisc Șirato (1871–1953). He grew up in the slums of Craiova in an environment that could be described as rural rather than urban but which provided his 'first initiation in art; this came from looking at *troitze* (wayside crosses) with their beautifully coloured saints in the vicinity of the fountain'.[9] (Later in his career Șirato befriended an old printer who taught him lithography and as a result he received a commission in 1897 to produce a colour poster from a popular book by Traian Demetrescu entitled *The Way We Love*; it was the first poster ever printed in Romania.[10])

It was during this era that a number of foreign painters who happened to be passing through Romania, as well as Romanian painters from other parts of the country, descended on Craiova, attracted to the town by the generous patronage of its prosperous bourgeoisie. Among them were Rossi di Giustiniani and A. V. Leopold Durand Durangel, from Italy and France respectively, while the Romanian painters included Eugenia Ștefan, Constantin Zaman, Constantin Alexianu and Ioan B. Dumitrescu.

On his own mean arrival in Craiova, Brancusi had been obliged to take up work as a waiter at a railway tavern owned by the Spirtaru brothers. There

I stayed six years and I was working an eighteen-hour shift every day. At three in the morning the carriage drivers woke me up by knocking with the handle of their whips on the door of the room where I was sleeping. They were coming to pick up their clients arriving on the early morning trains and before leaving with their cargo they wanted to be served hot sausages, cold white wine and hot horseradish.[11]

But in 1894 his situation changed radically for the better. He found employment in an upmarket provisions store in the town's commercial

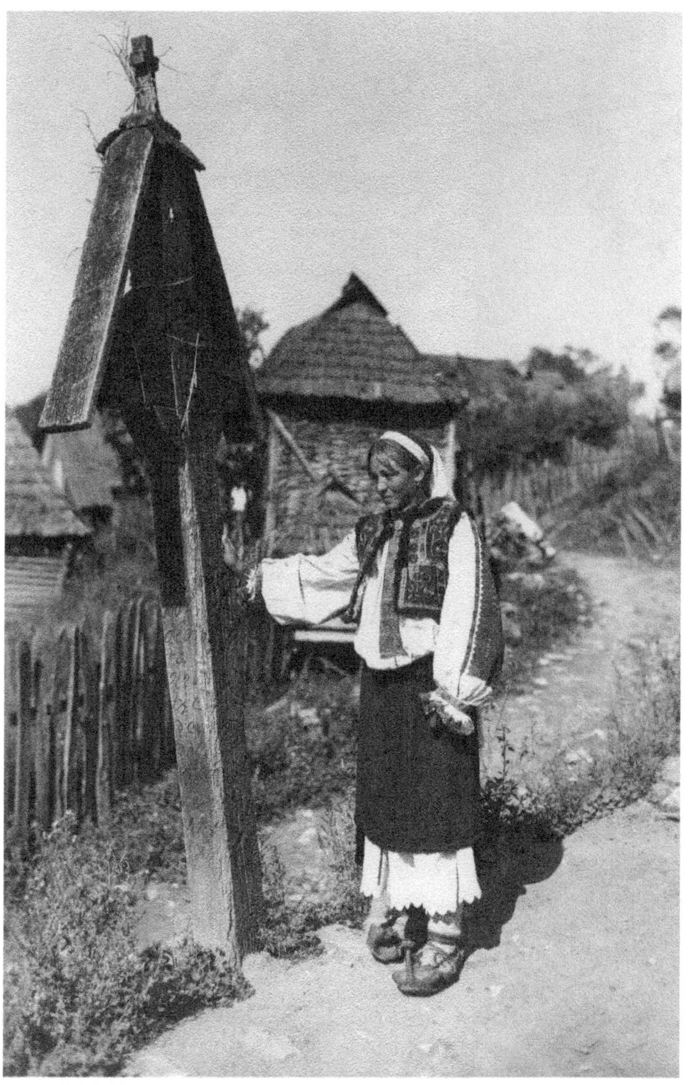

A girl by a wayside cross (*troiţă*) at Pădureni in Romania, early 20th century. The function of these often elaborately carved *troiţe* was commemorative or votive, providing for the weary traveller a place to pause, rest and pray.

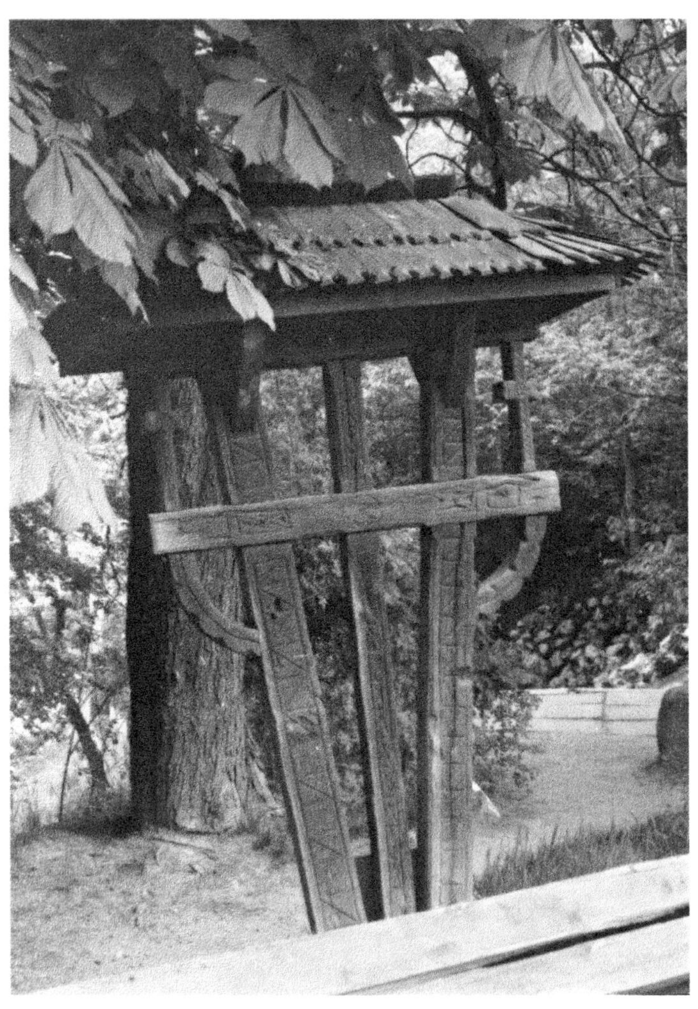

A *troiță* at the side of the road in Romania.

centre. Its owner, Ioan Zamfirescu, was the proud purveyor of
'fine wines and spirits' to the newly emerging local entrepreneurial
bourgeoisie, and Brancusi made himself popular with its well-heeled
clientele by his willingness to meet any challenge, however far-fetched:

> One day, someone challenged him to construct a violin, and bets
> were laid on the project. He took a wooden orange crate, cut it
> into thin, flexible slats, submitted them to a long boiling process
> in order to obtain the curves of the violin, procured some strings
> and rosin and soon completed his handiwork. A gypsy fiddler
> was called in to try it out, and to everyone's astonishment he
> charmed the audience with the purity of the tones emitted by
> the young prodigy's instrument.[12]

A rich manufacturer by the name of Grecescu, who was also the local
counsellor, witnessed this extraordinary event and remarked it would
be a pity for such talent to 'perish' and not 'go further', and therefore
that young Constantin should be placed in 'our school',[13] by which he
meant the local School of Arts and Crafts. With additional financial
help from the church of Madonna Dudu in Craiova, Brancusi began
at the School in September of the same year. (It has been suggested
that when Brancusi first arrived in Craiova he was illiterate, but that
on starting at this School he rapidly taught himself to read and write
in order to be able to catch up with his classmates and follow the
courses.[14])

Founded in 1871 as the Industrial School for Mechanical Arts,
Craiova's School of Arts and Crafts became one of Europe's pioneer-
ing institutions for industrial training; by 1894 it was called the School
of Arts and Crafts. The establishment of comparable schools of arts
and crafts in other major Romanian towns, including Bucharest,
enabled the country to take part in Europe's Universal Exhibitions,
which originated in London with the Great Exhibition of 1851.
(Romania had participated at London, but at that time had to

exhibit in the Turkish Pavilion, since politically it was still under Turkish suzeraneinty.[15])

The comprehensive syllabus of the School in Craiova offered training in 26 areas of technical and professional expertise, including foundry-work, blacksmithing, tailoring, shoemaking, metallurgy and agricultural mechanics as well sculpture, which in this context could be better described as decorative rather than artistic. A cursory look at the inventory of the artefacts produced by former alumni preserved in its museum gives an indication of the kind of objects Brancusi would have been trained to produce. Emphasis was on furniture and household merchandise: sideboards, desks, chairs, chandeliers, lamps, tables.[16] Brancusi himself is alleged to have made a number of such artefacts preserved in the School's museum, including a loom, two picture frames, a lotto set consisting of 90 pieces, a casket and a rather unusual corner chair in oak.[17]

During the summer of 1897, prior to his final year of study, Brancusi visited Vienna.[18] Nothing is known about his time there apart from the fact that he worked in a furniture factory and returned to Craiova with a 'qualification' certificate that confirmed his work experience.[19] It has been suggested that the furniture factory where he acquired this certificate was none other than the famous Maison Thonet, set up in Vienna in the mid-nineteenth century, where the important process of shaping bentwood veneers for furniture-making was developed.[20]

Brancusi completed his studies at the School of Arts and Crafts in 1898, and was able to exhibit one of his works in public at the Regional Exhibition of the Counties of Oltenia that took place in Craiova's 'Bibescu' Park. This was a prestigious show, part of a programme of public events organized in the town in order to enable people to become acquainted with painting, sculpture and the applied arts. The first such event was the Industrial Exhibition that took place in October 1869, where paintings by the famous painter Theodor Aman (one of the founders of the Academy of Fine Arts in Bucharest) could be admired alongside local artists. This was followed by an exhibition organized by the Craiova Society for the Education of the Romanian People held in the main *aula* of the Craiova Lyceum in 1873, followed in 1887 by the third exhibition organized by the Society of Cooperatives of Romania. In the section dedicated to the Fine Arts, Romania's most distinguished artists, mostly trained in Paris, including the painters Theodor Aman and Nicolae Grigorescu as well as the sculptor Ioan Georgescu (who was later to be Brancusi's professor in Bucharest), could be seen side by side with Craiova's own Rossi di Giustiniani, Nicolae Rădulescu and Constantin Stravolca.[21]

These events culminated in 1898 with the Regional Exhibition of the Counties of Oltenia, when Brancusi, then aged just 22, exhibited for the first time a plaster bust (since lost) of Gheorghe Chiţu (1828–1897). Chiţu had founded the Craiova School of Arts and Crafts during his time as a government minister, and its current director, Petre Popescu, who wanted to honour him, commissioned Brancusi to execute Chiţu's portrait using a photograph displayed in the staff room.[22]

That same year Brancusi completed his studies at the School of Arts and Crafts. Popescu wrote that his young pupil 'completed with great success the full theoretical and practical courses of five years of the school, in the sculpture section, having at the same time a great ability both in practical and theoretical studies as well as exemplary behaviour'.[23] The following term Brancusi enrolled at the Academy of Fine Arts in Romania's capital city, Bucharest.

3

Bucharest and the Academy
of Fine Arts

Brancusi arrived in Bucharest in 1898 to become a student of sculpture
at the Academy of Fine Arts. He was to remain there for the next four
years.[1] Still very poor, he was soon obliged to sell what little he had
inherited in order to survive. 'To study in the capital, I sold my share
of my parental inheritance. Radu Brâncuşi I think would turn in his
grave with shame and indignation. If he could have turned into a
ghost he would have strangled me, because I brought shame on the
family with the sale of my share.'[2] He also began washing dishes at
the Oswald restaurant in Câmpina Street, sharing the chores with
his new friend, Daniel Poiană.[3] Brancusi went on to befriend a few
other students, notably Ion Croitoru and Petre Neagoe, and it was
the latter who became his biographer. Here Neagoe remembers
Brancusi's daily routine:

At the first gleam of dawn Constantin arose, washed in cold
water in front of his door and took a turn in the garden. Then
he would light the fire in the kitchen stove, warm some milk
and have breakfast. At eight o'clock his landlady brewed Turkish
coffee and brought him a small cupful. She would place the coffee
on the table, make his bed and ask him how his sculpture was
getting on. The lump of clay on a large table took on a new shape
every day, but she could never figure out what he was trying to
make. Mischievously, Constantin kept her guessing, changing
the shape every night when he returned from school.[4]

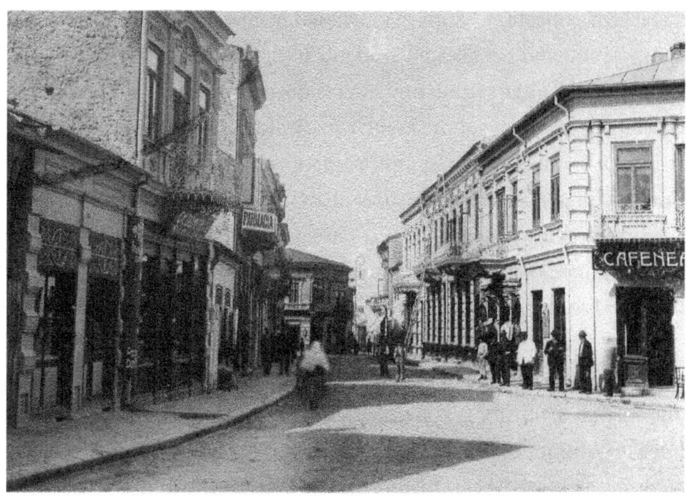

Lipscani Street, Bucharest, in the late 19th century.

Bucharest in the 1890s was a city of some 300,000 inhabitants. Although still a melting-pot where the traditional mingled with the modern and the urban with the rural, the colourful oriental scenes that had been enjoyed by hardy travellers and artists just half a century earlier had rapidly faded away. The city was in the grip of rapid change. The richly ornamented houses *à la Turque* were fast disappearing,[5] although parts of Bucharest continued to give the impression of being 'a park adorned by villas'.[6] An Academy of Fine Art had been founded there in 1865, five years after one had been established in the Moldavian capital of Jassy. Both were based on the French model. Bucharest's first director of the School of Painting was Theodor Aman (1831–1891), while Gheorghe M. Tăttărescu (1818–1894) was placed in charge of its curriculum.[7] The first professor of the School of Sculpture was the German-born sculptor Karl Storck (1826–1887).

An important aspect of these two academies was that they were each endowed with a *pinacotheca*, an art collection that doubled as a teaching collection.[8] Subjects included perspective, anatomy, composition and colour, and students in the School of Sculpture 'would model after statues and after nature', revealing Tăttărescu's thorough knowledge of the French curriculum. The five-year degree courses were in painting, sculpture, architecture and printmaking. The teaching included the history of art, perspective, anatomy, calligraphy and drawing.

In the case of sculpture, first-year students, whose ages ranged between fifteen and twenty-five, were taught to study after the antique (i.e., classical busts) and the history of art. During the second year the study after the antique continued with the full-length figure, anatomy and further art history. The third year incorporated clay modelling after the antique and after nature as well as the study of ornament, anatomy, perspective, art history and aesthetics. The fourth year included modelling after nature, composition, the study of drapery, anatomy, perspective, history of art and aesthetics. During the final year students were taught the study of figure *rondbosse*, portrait busts and composition.[9] Comparison with the curriculum on offer

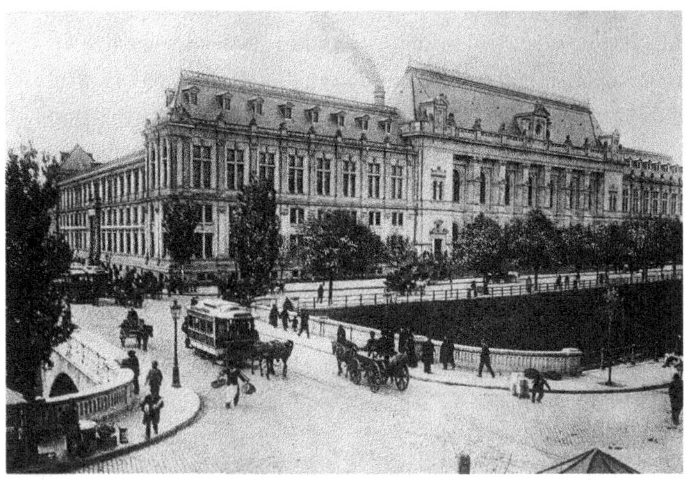

The Palace of Justice in Bucharest, in the early 20th century.

at the Ecole des Beaux-Arts in Paris reveals the extent to which the two Romanian academies were indebted to their French counterpart.

The transition from copying engravings to copying casts was known as *passing à la bosse, bosse* being the term employed during the nineteenth century for plaster-casts. Technically this constituted the intermediary stage between drawing from engravings to drawing after the live model. Copying the cast was meant to increase awareness of tri-dimensionality, and consequently the casts were chosen from classical examples in order to increase students' awareness of the importance of antiquity.[10]

As a student at the Academy of Fine Arts, Brancusi was expected to go through this rigorous process of artistic education. Although very little is known about his student years, he would have complied with the rigours of the curriculum, which helps us to understand better the theoretical and practical instruction he chose to absorb. More importantly, although his craft studies at Craiova probably left him ill-prepared for art schooling at Bucharest, the training he received in the capital did set him up thoroughly for Paris, not least because it was based on the canonical French system.

When the School had first been set up, and aware of the lack of available teaching material, Theodor Aman, who had trained in Paris, used his French contacts to order a number of plaster-casts from the Louvre that included the portrait bust of the Roman emperor Vitellius and various Hellenistic masterpieces, among them the *Venus de Milo*, the *Gladiator*, the *Apollo Belvedere* and the *Laocoön* group. In 1869 Karl Storck had been dispatched to Italy on a mission to select the plaster-casts he considered necessary for academic study. His choices show his Hellenistic preferences: *Child with a Goose*, a bust of Ajax, *Child with Eagle*, *Venus at her Toilette* and a bas-relief representing Medusa.[11]

In spite of these modest beginnings, the total lack of illustrative material as well as reproductions of works from Western European museums, notwithstanding Theodor Aman's relentless effort to address it, continued to constitute a challenge to the ambitious programme of the Academy. Thus in 1872 an album with engravings representing the archaeological discoveries from Pompeii and Herculaneum on display at the Archaeological Museum of Naples was bought and reprinted in Romania.[12]

The scarcity of visual material available to students was however being complemented from an unexpected and hitherto unresearched source. An independent Romanian press, by then about a century old, was producing an impressive number of publications dedicated to general knowledge as well as those that were more specialized.[29] It is likely that popular magazines such as *Tribuna Familiei*, which began in October 1898, and the more ambitious *Noua Revista Romana*, first published in 1900,[13] which covered politics and literature as well as the arts, would not have escaped Brancusi's attention. The 1900 Universal Exhibition in Paris was given extensive coverage in two consecutive issues of the *Noua Revista Romana*.

Ion Georgescu (1856–1898) and Stefan Ionescu-Valbudea (1856–1918) were among the first to become students of sculpture in the class of Karl Storck at the Academy's Faculty of Sculpture. After completing the arduous five-year course both of them obtained scholarships to study in Paris, where they distinguished themselves by winning prizes for their work exhibited at the Paris Salon. Thus Georgescu's lyrical sculptures influenced by neo-classicism entitled *The Source*, *Girl Praying* and *Endymion Hunting* were exhibited in Paris, with *Girl Praying* receiving an honourable mention. Like Auguste Rodin in Paris and, much later, Jacob Epstein in London, Georgescu became a fashionable portrait sculptor to high society in Bucharest after his success with the portrait of Pascaly, mentioned above, executed immediately after his death in 1882.

Equally generous with his knowledge, Georgescu became professor of sculpture at the Academy of Fine Arts in 1887, where he worked until his untimely death at the age of forty-two in 1898, the year in which Brancusi became a student. For a short time, until 30 November

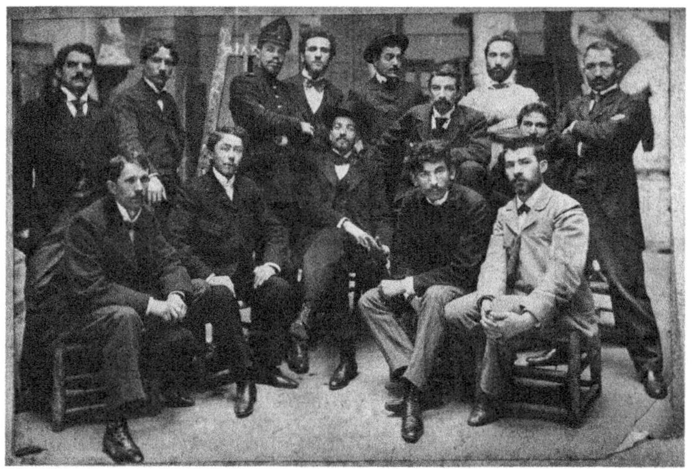

Brancusi (front row, far right) with fellow students at the Academy of Fine Arts, Bucharest, *c.* 1901.

1898, Georgescu taught Brancusi, after which the young student switched to Vladimir Hegel (1839–1918).

Another important development Brancusi would have profited from on his arrival in Bucharest was the founding of institutions and venues dedicated to supporting the visual arts, complemented by the emergence of an impressive culture of collecting and patronage. Bucharest boasted collectors such as Krikor H. Zambaccian (1889–1962) and Anastase Simu (1854–1935), both of whom were almost certainly comparable with Sergei Schukin and Ivan Morozov in Moscow. Simu was the discerning individual who later commissioned the beautiful marble head *Sleep* from Brancusi in 1908 when the sculptor was still completely unknown.[14]

At some point during his time at the Academy Brancusi was persuaded by his friend and fellow student Ion Croitoru to join him as a member of a church choir, and as a chorister Brancusi learned both Gregorian and Byzantine chant.[15] It was to Croitoru that Brancusi appears to have left a sketchbook bound in red cloth with the title on

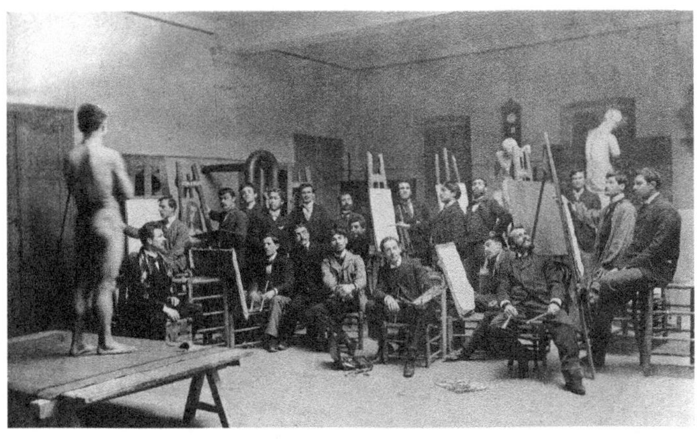

Students at the Academy of Fine Arts in 1900.

the cover 'Schiţe C. Brâncuşi', although his authorship of these sketches has since been disputed.[16] Their subject-matter, which includes townscapes, the human figure, self-portraits, mycology and studies of both the nude and human osteology,[17] reflect, as do the sculptures Brancusi made during his student years in Bucharest (both extant as well as those known only from photographs), the rigorous academic training he underwent at the Academy.

Students were recommended to keep sketchbooks of the sort allegedly given to Croitoru. Antoine Etex, author of a *Course élementaire de dessin* (1877), advised that, like a painting, a drawing 'cannot be done straight off':

A notebook sketch is done in this way and the skilful artist may put a great deal into a drawing tossed off in this manner. But the pupil must go to work more humbly, starting with simple elements and working up to more complex, keeping the main aim in view and achieving delicacy by degrees without losing sight of the mass.[18]

The number of works made by Brancusi during this period that were either lost or destroyed and are known only from photographs exceed that of the surviving body, which consists of four works. One is a life-size statue of a flayed man in multiple versions – the *Ecorché*, commissioned by his professor of anatomy Dr Dimitrie Gerota for didactic purposes. It was modelled after the so-called Capitoline *'Antinous'* (now known to be a Roman copy of a Greek *Hermes*). The final result was a demonstration of Brancusi's technical ability as well as scientific accuracy. He was forced to undertake research at the morgue for this commission, and perhaps his well-known revulsion for human anatomy might have been instilled by this experience.[19]

The other three comprise a plaster bust of *Vitellius*, and a bust portrait each of Dr Carol Davila and Brancusi's friend from Craiova, Ion Georgescu-Gorjan, whose son, Stefan, was later to play a seminal part in the construction of the *Column without End* in Tîrgu-Jiu.[20] Photographs of ten lost or destroyed works include a plaster study of *Laöcoon*, a life-size relief of *Mars Borghese*, two studies of women's heads, a male nude, a study of a public monument (*Allegory*), and two anatomical studies as well as the original plaster version of the *Ecorché*.[21]

Brancusi graduated in April 1902, and between April and November of that year was obliged to complete his military service, although he continued to attend practical courses at the Academy and was allowed to make use there of the workshop facilities. On 24 September he received his Diploma number Two. He then applied to the church of Madonna Dudu in Craiova – which had generously supported him throughout his studies in Craiova as well as in Bucharest – for a grant to enable him to study in Italy.[22] But his wish was not granted. So he took the advice of his friend Dimitrie Paciurea (1875–1932), a vastly talented sculptor virtually unknown outside Romania, who had recently spent several years (1895–1900) in Paris on a state scholarship. Paciurea was the maker of an uncanny series of sculptures, *The Chimeras*, and it is possible that Brancusi's

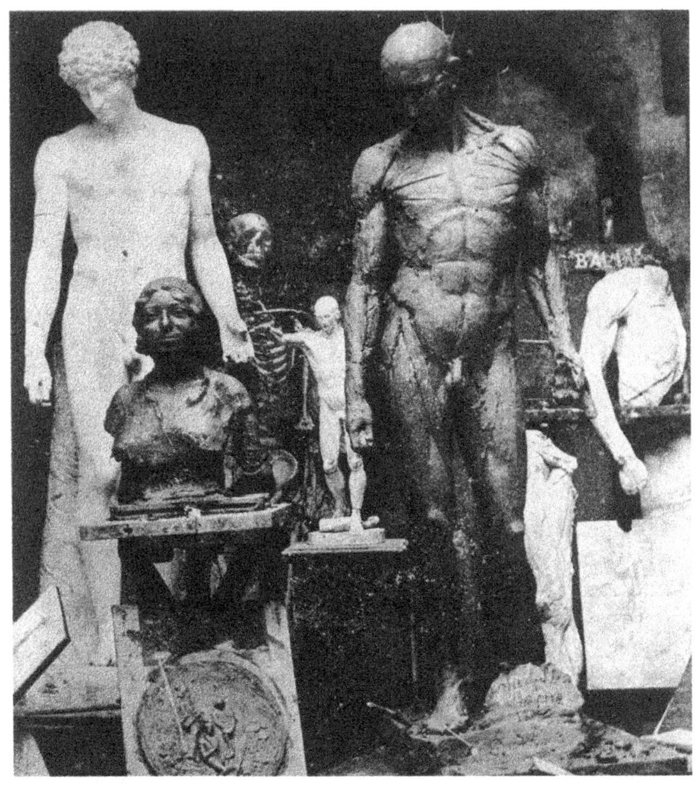

Academy of Fine Arts, Bucharest, 1901, student work including the *écorché* (centre) executed by Brancusi in terracotta at the request of his professor of anatomy, Dimitrie Gerota. This work was after the plaster copy (far left) of the famous *'Antinous Capitolinus'* discovered in the remains of Hadrian's Villa, Tivoli, that was among the copies belonging to the study collection at the Academy.

own wooden *Chimera* made in 1915–18 may have been inspired at least at a conceptual level by Paciurea's earlier work.[23] Paciurea told Brancusi to head for Munich.

Very little is known about the relationship between these two. They first met after Paciurea's return from Paris, and it was Paciurea who first introduced Brancusi to the avant-garde association Tinerimea

Artistica ('Artistic Youth'). Its first exhibition was held in 1902 when
Queen Elizabeth, who wrote also poetry under the *nom-de-plume*
'Carmen Sylva', was the guest of honour. Tinerimea Artistica was
to play an important part in Brancusi's early artistic career, and his
contributions to their exhibitions, at which he showed regularly
between 1907 and 1914, is well documented.

The Munich that Paciurea directed Brancusi towards in 1902
was then a city that was home to various progressive trends in art,
including Art Nouveau. Brancusi probably reached the Bavarian
capital in the summer of 1903.[24] He met up with his friend there, the
sculptor Frederich Storck, who helped him out. He passed the winter
months visiting museums, frequenting the famous Hofbräuhaus and
other beer-halls where artists gathered, taking walks through the city
and its parks and gardens, and looking for work, though he found
none. He later admitted that the Munich he encountered didn't really
appeal to him, one of the reasons being that he seemed unable to
learn German. In addition, he realized that the kind of training given
at the school of fine art there, the Akademie der Bildenden Künste,
was too similar to that which he had already received in Bucharest.
So, one fine spring day in 1904, he set off for Paris.[25]

4

Paris

Brancusi arrived in Paris on 14 July after a lengthy hike from Munich,[1] a journey he later recounted in his own rhapsodic manner:

> I walked along the country roads. I rambled through forests singing my joy and in the villages I was given food and drink. The peasants welcomed me with open arms, gave me provisions and wished me a pleasant journey. They realized that I was one of them. Sometimes I would pause in the fields in which cows were peacefully grazing. I'd whistle the old tunes from my country. One day I saw a cow stop grazing to listen to my song. I was enchanted. But when I looked a little closer, I realized she was simply . . . making water. It was then that I understood the vanity of fame.[2]

The Paris that Brancusi reached in 1904 was a renewed metropolis of Haussmannian boulevards and the iconic Eiffel Tower built for the Universal Exhibition of 1889. He arrived during the infancy of the Metro system, on which work had started in the late 1890s, with the first lines effective in 1900. Its entrances, with their Art Nouveau balustrades and elaborate signage – elegant organic forms based on variations on the theme of foliage – by the architect Hector Guimard, were proliferating across the capital. We will see similar forms emerging in Brancusi's languid series of ovoids.

It was, however, the Universal Exhibition of 1900 that ushered in modernity (to which Romania was not only an enthusiastic but also an

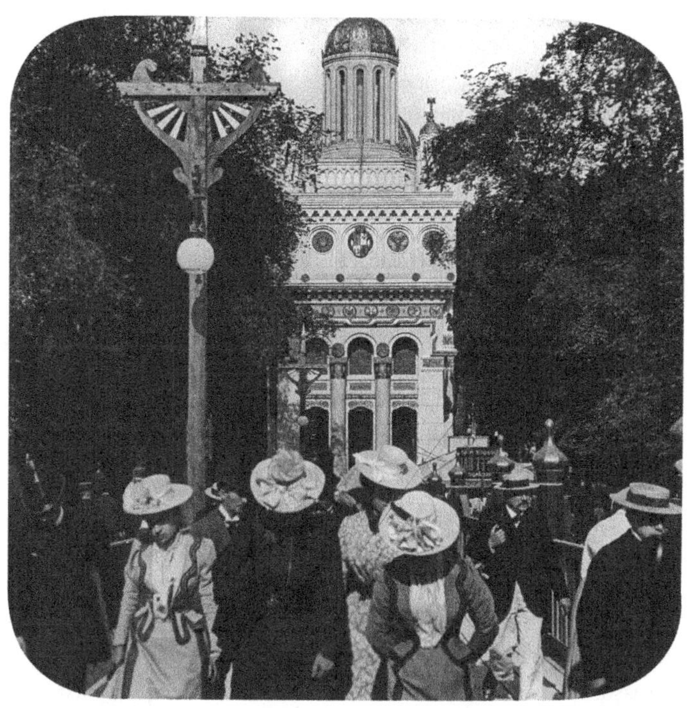

The Romanian Pavilion (architect Jean-Camille Formigé) at the Universal Exhibition of 1900 held in Paris.

ambitious participant), and between that date and 1937, the year of the last Universal Exhibition, Paris was the unchallenged cultural capital of Europe. Even more impressive in scale than any of the previous shows, the fourth Universal Exhibition of 1900 bequeathed to the capital city both the neo-Baroque Grand Palais and Petit Palais, built next to each other on a vast triangle of ground separating the Champs-Elysées and the River Seine's right bank, and near to them the magnificent Pont Alexandre III, which reached over the Seine to the Quai d'Orsay on an alignment with the Hôtel des Invalides beyond.

At that time two major artistic communities existed side by side in Paris, at Montmartre and Montparnasse. They provided the fertile ground that became the cradle of the avant-garde movements inaugurated with Fauvism (located in Montmartre) in 1905. Montmartre became famous for its nightlife: clubs, dance-halls and cafés-concerts such as the Moulin de la Galette, Moulin Rouge and Chat Noir.[3] Above all, Le Lapin Agile became the meeting-place for artists living in the studios located at 13 rue Ravignan, better known as 'Le Bâteau-Lavoir' (the laundry boat) because of its distinctive ugliness. The Bâteau-Lavoir was the place in which Picasso established himself after several years of shifts back and forth between Paris and Barcelona. Both Brancusi and Picasso made Paris their home in 1904.

The history of Montmartre's bohemia begins earlier than *la bande à Picasso* and the Bâteau-Lavoir, stretching back to 1869 when the district became the 18th *arrondissement* of Paris. The first colony of artists that settled there were the Nouvelle Athènes, which included Thomas Couture, Puvis de Chavannes, Jonkind and Alfred Stevens.[4] The special association between the aristocratic Henri de Toulouse-Lautrec and the Moulin Rouge ensured that the cabaret venue subsequently became the quintessential home for the free-spirited life associated with bohemia. The Bal du Moulin Rouge opened in 1889 at 90 boulevard de Clichy in the Pigalle district close to Montmartre, and its red illuminated windmill dominating its surroundings, as well as its motley international dancers, clowns and assorted cabaret performers, became the area's most recognizable landmark. This *désuet* crowd performing in or gravitating to the Bal du Moulin Rouge was immortalized by Toulouse-Lautrec, who had been living in the area since the mid-1880s.

Montmartre was a decadent, free-spirited, poor but irreverent world that functioned like a magnet. Little wonder that Erik Satie, Brancusi's future close friend, chose Montmartre as his first artistic habitat. In 1887 Satie was renting a room in rue Condorcet, close to Cirque Medrano; a year later Rodolphe Salis, the owner of the Chat Noir, hired Satie to play piano at his establishment. Satie reinvented himself accordingly by morphing into a proper bohemian. He moved

to rue Cortot just behind the popular place de Tertre, changed
the spelling of his name from Eric to Erik, and, in keeping with
his new status of serious composer, grew a beard and took to
wearing a pince-nez, a flowing tie, a velvet coat and a soft felt hat.[5]

Picasso's decision in 1904 to set up his studio in the Bâteau-Lavoir
was to be instrumental in Montmartre's continuing reputation into
the twentieth century as the locus of the birth of the first avant-garde
movements, Fauvism and Cubism. After working through his Blue
and Pink periods he embarked in 1907 on what is now seen as one
of the most iconic works of European modernism, *Les Demoiselles
d'Avignon*. Max Jacob, Guillaume Apollinaire and Fernande Olivier
were among the new presences in his life – *la bande à Picasso* – who
congregated at Le Lapin Agile, a place that was reckoned especially
attractive in the summer-time. Picasso would 'bring his dogs and
sit on the rustic terrace in the shade of the acacia tree in whose
branches the proprietor's monkey would play, while Lolo, his artistic
donkey, ate everything in sight.'[6] Over the years new members of
la Bande included Braque, Derain, Vlaminck, Valadon, Modigliani,
Gris, Herbin, Marcoussis, Utrillo and Marie Laurencin. Even the
unbohemian Matisse paid the occasional visit.[7]

Montparnasse, on the other hand, was still a gentrified village
even at the beginning of the twentieth century. Its transformation
into a modern arrondissement didn't begin until 1905, when the
majority of the two-storey houses on the boulevard du Montparnasse
were replaced by modern buildings. Before then, as Modigliani's
companion, Roger Wild, recalled, one still found farms 'with cows,
pigs, horses and hens' in Montparnasse, one such being 'Nourrissons'
in rue de Fleurus,[8] the quiet street just west of the Jardin de Luxem-
bourg in which Leo and Gertrude Stein settled in 1903 (at number
27) and established a popular salon.

Like Montmartre, Montparnasse also offered a variety of entertainment, especially theatres, such as the Montparnasse and Gaîté-
Montparnasse, and the popular music-halls, which included Bobino

in rue de la Gaîté.[9] A considerably more intellectual equivalent of
the picturesque Le Lapin Agile was the high-brow establishment La
Closerie des Lilas, which became a gathering place for ontparnasse's
bohemians and also the meeting-place of the improvised editorial
board of Paul Fort's magazine *Vers et Prose*. (In 1953 La Closerie
des Lilas – by then an exclusive restaurant – celebrated 150 years
of business, but this elegant establishment was nothing like the
modest café Fort had chosen as his office for producing the magazine.) Although *Vers et Prose* initially attracted mostly writers and
poets (Verlaine, Strindberg, Wilde and Maeterlinck were all regular
contributors), they were later replaced by visual artists, some of
whom emigrated from Montmartre to the Left Bank. By 1912 La
Closerie des Lilas was the main gathering-place for artists both from
Montmartre and Montparnasse: Bourdelle, Vlaminck, Braque,
Léger, Modigliani, Brancusi and many others could be found there.[10]

On his arrival in Paris Brancusi lodged first with his friend from
Bucharest, Daniel Poiană, at 9 cité Condorcet near Montmartre,
and Poiană found him a job washing dishes at the Brasserie Chartier.
Brancusi later remembered this episode as one during which he
gave to the world of catering his unique contribution to efficient
kitchen hygiene:[11]

> I worked to start with in order to earn my living as a dish-washer
> in restaurants. I was a sort of glass-washer. I did not pour to the
> clients. I was specializing in washing glasses. I did even come
> up with an invention to enable me to wash them faster. Until
> I arrived glasses were washed twice, once in hot and once in cold
> water. I suppressed the cold water and was only using boiling hot
> water. Hot water was dissolving grease, it was hygienic and the
> glasses dried faster. It was burning the tips of my rough fingers
> but I resigned myself to it.[12]

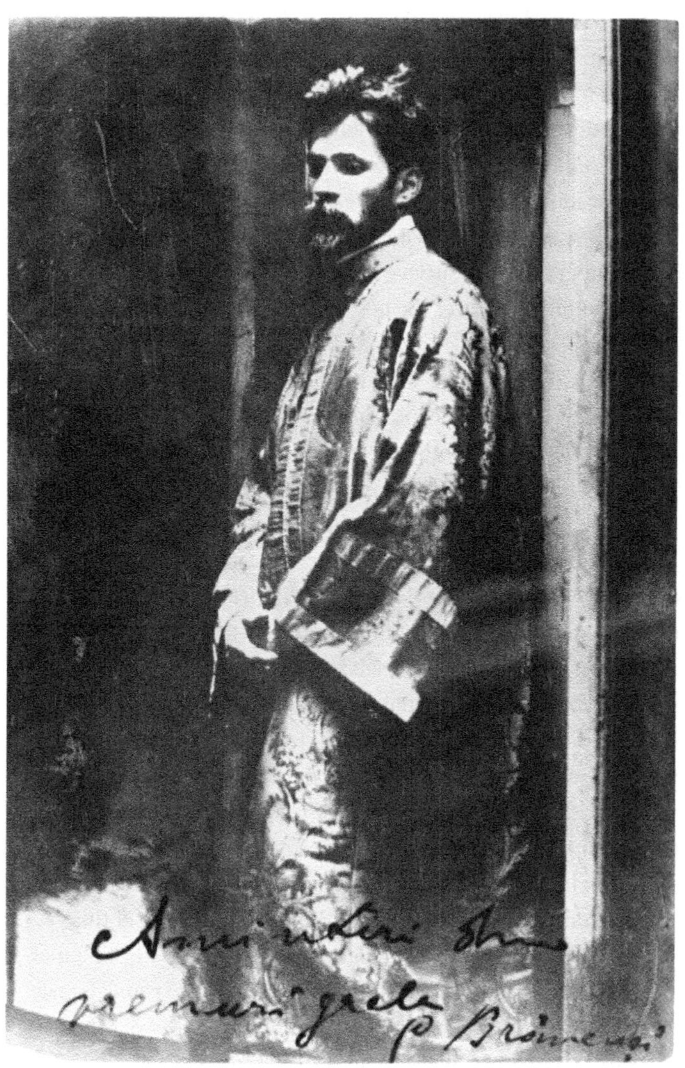

Brancusi in sacristan attire in 1906.

He changed home several times over the next three years. In March 1905 he moved to 10 place de la Bourse, then to 16 place Dauphine (both in Montparnasse) and in 1907, as a consequence of a lucrative commission, to the more salubrious 54 rue du Montparnasse in the heart of bohemia.[13] A small grant from Romania's Ministry of Arts and Education enabled him to register as a student at the Ecole des Beaux-Arts, and he attended classes there at Anton Mercié's studio. The photographs that survive to show works (many now lost) that Brancusi undertook over the next two or three years reveal that many were portrait busts in bronze. He was working in an academic style on busts that include a charming series of children, of which he produced multiple versions and variations – *The Child*, the *Head of a Child*, *Torment* and others.[14]

More unusual were the bronze *Portrait of the Painter Nicolae Dărăscu* of 1906 and *Sleep* (1908), the latter a lyrical head carved in marble commissioned by the collector Anastase Simu for his private museum in Bucharest. For the bronze of his friend Dărăscu, Brancusi employed for the first time, following Rodin's method of fragmentation, the 'partial figure', which enabled him to eliminate parts of the anatomy for expressive purposes. This new approach invented by Rodin became a well-established technique popular with avant-garde sculptors, and it was adopted by Brancusi too. In the *Nicolae Dărăscu*, which is closely related to the *Torment* series, Brancusi started to experiment with the 'partial figure' by eliminating his right arm, a technique he perfected in his first modernist masterpiece, *The Prayer*.

The exact relationship between Brancusi and Rodin at this stage borders on the apocryphal, but it is likely that they first met when Brancusi had the good fortune to befriend two young female Romanian writers, Otilia Cosmutza and Marie Bengesco. Moreover, Brancusi became, according to his own testimony, Rodin's pupil, albeit for a short time.

Otilia Cosmutza (1874–1951) was a journalist who contributed articles for the Romanian art magazine *Luceafărul*, where she was the first to report on Brancusi's work in Paris. Between 1907 and 1914 she was the secretary of the distinguished novelist Anatole France. Her second marriage, to the Hungarian writer Gyorgy Bölöny, took her to Budapest, where in 1924 she published her memoirs under the title *Promenades avec Anatole France*.[15] Marie Bengesco (1850–1936) had trained at the Ecole du Louvre, specializing in the history of French furniture. She had been a close friend of Rodin for decades. (In 1919 she was to contribute an essay, 'L'Art roumain', for *La Roumanie en images,* in which she provides a brief but astute analysis of Brancusi's sculpture.) It was, however, Cosmutza who was instrumental in introducing Brancusi to Rodin. An entry in her diary for 3 January 1907 records that 'During the evening [I was] in my room with four bouquets of violets'. Three had been given her by some little girls, but the fourth was from Brancusi, 'who was waiting with it in front of my gate. I had not seen Brancusi since we went together to Meudon to visit Rodin.'[16] It is likely that this first meeting with Rodin at the Villa des Brillants, which had been the famous sculptor's Meudon suburban retreat since 1895, occurred in December 1906. As a consequence of their acquaintance, Brancusi spent a period working under Rodin at the latter's studio in the rue de l'Université:

> I became a pupil in Rodin's studio, where I reached a great technical dexterity. I was making a sculpture each day in the style of Rodin. I could no longer live near him although he loved me. I was imitating him. I was unconsciously being a pasticheur but I could see the pastiche. I was miserable. These were the most difficult years, years of searching, years of seeking my own path. I had to leave Rodin. I upset him but I had to find my own path. I arrived at simplicity, peace and joy through my own intimate difficulties.[17]

To what extent Brancusi was really unhappy during his brief apprenticeship to Rodin is harder to ascertain than Rodin's overwhelming influence on the young Romanian's style, especially at the juncture when Brancusi abandoned the safe academic style of working for which the Bucharest Academy had prepared him for the intermediary period of expressionist modelling and the use of the 'partial figure'.

In 1907, thanks to the Romanian diaspora in Paris, Brancusi obtained his first major commission. It came from a wealthy widow, Eliza Stănescu-Popovici, and was to be a memorial to her recently departed husband. According to the contract, signed on 18 April, Brancusi undertook to 'erect in Buzău for the sum of 7,500 *lei* (the Romanian currency) a funerary monument, consisting of an allegorical figure of a weeping woman, and a bust with arms and a base'.[18] The sketch predictably consists of a *pleureuse* sprawled prostrate in distress on a three-step pedestal before a plinth, on which was to be placed a bust portrait of the deceased. But the final result was something quite different: instead of a *pleureuse* – of which Romanian cemeteries were full – Brancusi produced a daring image of a kneeling woman praying, with one arm missing. He later recalled how the idea of placing a naked woman in a cemetery might have been offensive and instead he decided to produce 'a prayer' instead by transforming the praying woman into an abstraction – literally *a prayer*. Brancusi 's *The Prayer* is a monument that constituted such a radical departure not only from the established norms of funerary sculpture but also from representations of a nude human figure placed in a cemetery that it would at that time have provoked consternation in Paris, never mind small-town Buzau.

Over the years there has been much speculation regarding his sources of inspiration, but Brancusi was then looking not at other sculptures but at paintings, specifically those by Paul Cézanne.[19] In 1907 there were two extensive posthumous exhibitions of Cézanne's work, one at Galérie Bernheim-Jeune consisting of watercolours, and the second at the Salon d'Automne of 56 oil paintings. The latter show included two (of the three) versions of his magnificent large *Bathers*.

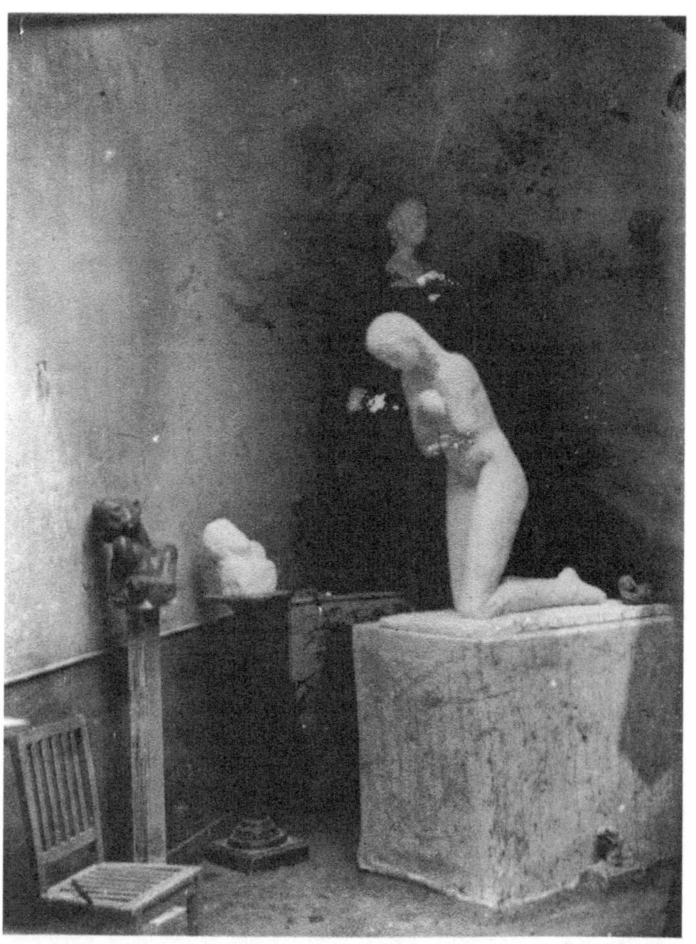

Brancusi's studio at 54 rue du Montparnasse with *The Prayer*, *c*. 1907, plaster.

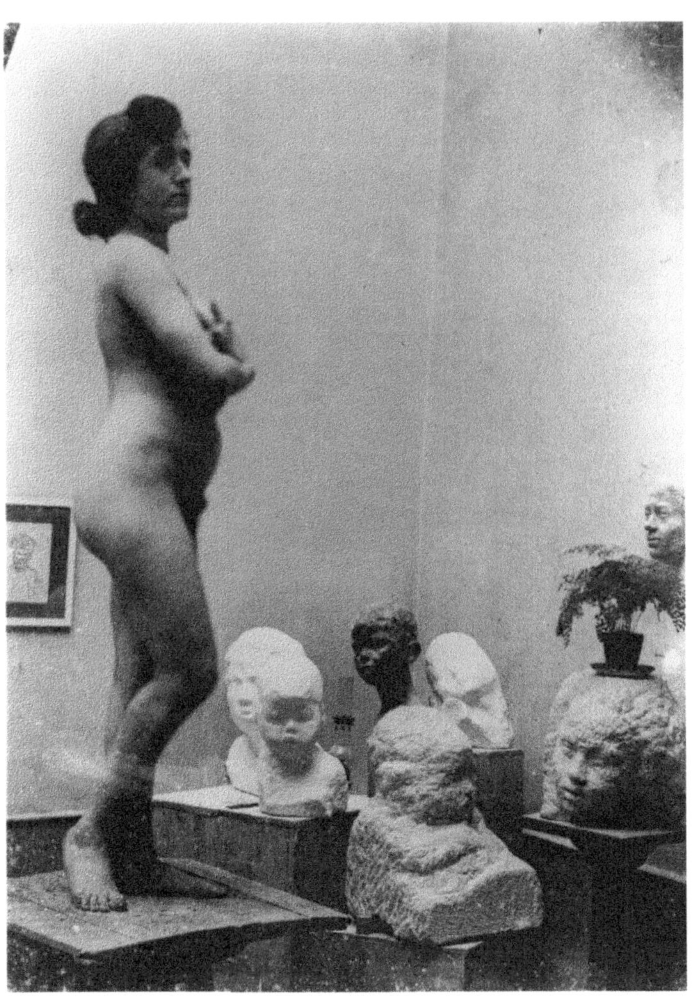

Brancusi's model, late 1907.

A comparison between Brancusi's kneeling figure and Cézanne's nude bathers reveals the extent to which the the young sculptor was under Cézanne's influence.

The original plaster version of *The Prayer* (since lost) is shown in the photograph (see page 49) that was taken in Brancusi's studio at 54 rue de Montparnasse,[20] the studio that *The Prayer* commission had enabled him to move to, and where he was remain for the next nine years.[21] The photograph reveals the stark poverty with which Brancusi had to contend during this period: a massive rectangular plinth for the praying figure; two modest stands for two versions of *Torment*, one in bronze and the other in marble (since lost), which may have been one of Brancusi's first attempts at direct carving, the technique that was to inform the first important series of works based on a motif – *The Kiss*. In another photograph (opposite) we see the naked dark-haired woman who was the model for *The Prayer*; she is on a sculptor's stand, her feet level with the tops of six other plinths bearing busts of children, on top of one of which Brancusi has playfully placed a potted plant.[22] Nothing seems to be known about the identity of the young model, but if we are to give credence to Peter Neagoe, she was Marthe, a young woman Brancusi met (when living at place Dauphine) at Le Lapin Agile, and whose generosity extended, in true bohemian fashion, to becoming his model, cook and mistress. As it is related in *The Saint of Montparnasse*, Brancusi 'accepted Marthe's abject devotion without thinking too much about it. It was an established order of things for a Parisian artist to have a mistress.'[23] No documentation exists to confirm her shadowy presence in Brancusi's life, a circumstance not helped by Brancusi's notorious refusal to discuss personal relationships.

Two well-documented feminine presences in Brancusi's life and career do appear in 1907 and 1910 respectively: Baroness Renée Frachon and the Hungarian painter Magit Pogany. It was Otilia Cosmutza who introduced the Baroness to Brancusi. The pair met regularly between 1908 and 1910, although the Baroness and her

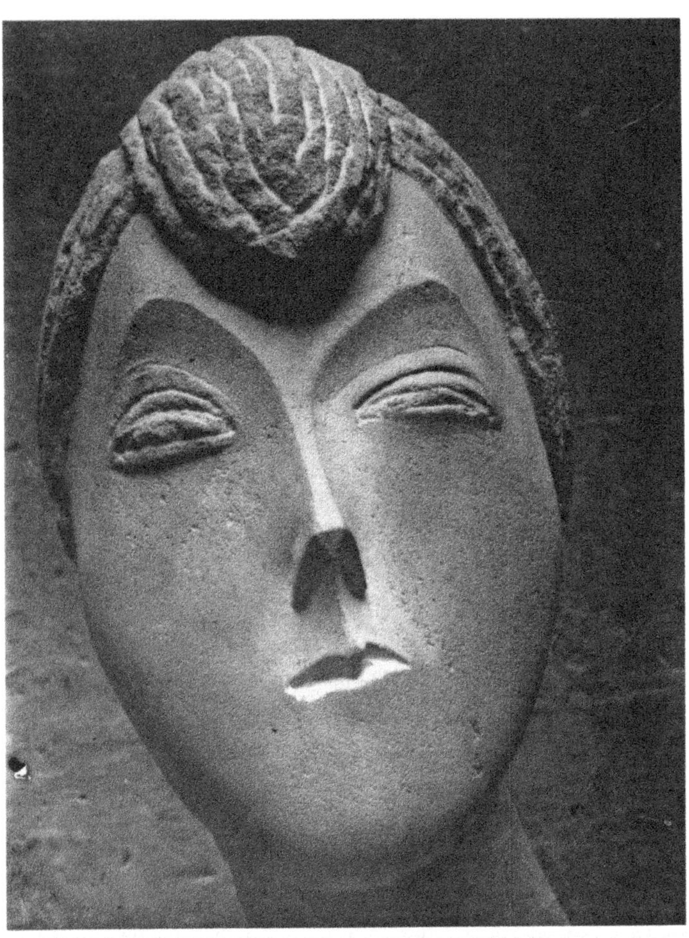

La Baronne R. F., 1909, stone (present location unknown). In 1907 Brancusi adopted a revolutionary new technique inspired by tribal art: direct carving. With the exception of the first version of *The Kiss,* generally accepted to be the half-length version in the Craiova Museum, all the other works executed in this technique are lost or were destroyed.

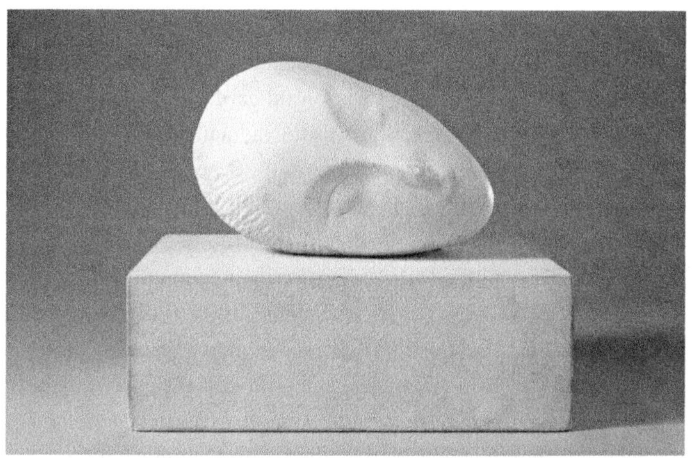

Sleeping Muse, 1909–10. This marble head in the Hirshhorn Museum and Sculpture Garden is the first in the series of ovoids Brancusi embarked on in 1909. The sculpture represents the Baroness Renée Frachon, the model for *La Baronne R. F.*

husband travelled extensively. The correspondence that ensued between them continued until Brancusi's death.[24] She first sat for him in 1908. The resulting series of *The Sleeping Muse* began with the beautiful marble version now in the Hirshhorn Museum and Sculpture Garden, Washington, DC, which signalled the beginning of a new phase in Brancusi's career: the motifs.

His first attempts at portraying his aristocratic sitter still complied with the Rodinesque approach of expressive modelling, as two photographs of a clay model reveal (now lost, dated 1908). The photographs first published in the Romanian magazines *Ramuri* and *Tribuna* in 1965 originate from the archives of Otilia Cosmutza.[25] It was at this point that Brancusi abandoned modelling and produced a stone-carved version of Renée Frachon's portrait (see opposite), variously dated 1909 or 1910 (lost, but known from photographs).[26] A comparison between the clay and stone versions, the latter for which Brancusi employed 'direct carving', provide a unique insight into

the otherwise poorly documented period of transition when Brancusi
made the radical move from academic strictures to become one of
the foremost sculptors among Paris's avant-garde.

Equally radical, if more subtle, was the reductionist method
employed within the multiple versions of the ovoid of *The Sleeping
Muse* through a methodical process of simplification whereby the
figurative elements were being gradually streamlined towards
abstraction. Thus, in the earliest versions the features are still
recognizably those of the Baroness. Around 1917 or 1918 however,
two new versions, *The Sleeping Muse II* dated 1920 and a *Sleeping
Muse III* of 1917–18, were made. The exact chronology between them
seems uncertain, but in *Sleeping Muse II*, which exists in two versions,
one alabaster and the other marble, the features, although more
generalized than in *Sleeping Muse III*, are also more focused.[27]

Brancusi's portrait versions of Margit Pogany, together with
Picasso's *Demoiselles d'Avignon*, are the most iconic signifiers of
Parisian Modernism with all its revolutionary implications, yet
in both instances their genesis appears to be shrouded in mystery.
Picasso's masterpiece was very likely completed in 1907, but he
decided to keep it back and it was not exhibited until 1916, although
even then neither friends nor the public were impressed. In 1922
the couturier and collector Jacques Doucet was brave enough to buy
the painting, and three years later André Breton published it in the
July issue of *La Révolution Surréaliste*. But it was not until 1937 that
the painting was properly shown to the public before being shipped
to America, where it remains.[28] Picasso was intensely aware of the
place of this painting in the hierarchy of things:

He had proved what he had set out to prove, that he was
Baudelaire's *peintre de la vie moderne*, but he was too far ahead
of the field to be perceived as such, hence a feeling of bitterness
rather than gratification.[29]

The circumstances of Brancusi's first meeting with Margit Pogany are obscure, but it appears to have taken place on 1 July 1910 when she visited his studio for the first time in the company of a friend.[30] According to Brancusi's Romanian friend V. G. Paleolog, 'Mlle Pogany was brought to Brancusi by Otilia Cosmutza, invited by Brancusi, who fell in love because of a particularity of her eyes'.[31] Paleolog added a mischievous description of Margit Pogany's physique:

> Proportioned with meanness, she disposed of her arms, which were longer than was necessary, and knowing this she kept them bent as often as possible, which suited her better in the same way as sitting on a chair either stiffly or lopsided, since her walk was ducklike.[32]

Much later, in 1952, Margit Pogany dated the first visit to Brancusi's studio to 1911, writing in a letter that Brancusi had invited her to see his work:

> I went with a friend of mine and he showed me his sculptures. Among them was a head of white marble which attracted me strongly. I felt it was me, although it had none of my features. It was all eyes.[33]

In a second letter, dated 4 August 1953, and addressed to Alfred H. Barr Jr, the director of MoMA in New York, she recanted these dates by stating that it was in July 1910 that she had visited Brancusi's studio for the first time, which was followed by sittings in December 1910 and January 1911, shortly after which she left Paris.[34] In her first letter she also had something to say about the sittings:

> I wished very much to have my portrait done by Brancusi and asked whether he would do it. He was greatly pleased by my proposal, would not discuss the financial side, saying anything

I should offer would be alright. . . . I sat for him several times.
Each time he began and finished a new bust in clay. Each of these
was a beautiful and a wonderful likeness, and each time he only
laughed and threw it back into the boxful of clay that stood in the
corner of the studio – to my great disappointment. Once I had to
sit for my hands but the pose was quite different to that of my
present bust, he only wanted to learn them by heart as he already
knew my head by heart.[35]

As with the case of *The Sleeping Muse*, in 1907 Brancusi was still
working in clay in tandem with his experiments in direct carving,
and in the case of the ovoids he started as a rule with a carving
and cast all the subsequent versions from it in bronze.

Again as with *The Sleeping Muse*, the same reductionist process is
employed in the multiple versions of *Mlle Pogany*, who is subjected
to a rigorous process of simplification starting from the earliest
multiple versions dated 1913 through to the multiple versions of
Mlle Pogany II and finally those of *Mlle Pogany III* of 1931.[36]

What distinguishes the portraits of Renée Frachon and Margit
Pogany is that in the case of the former the young aristocrat's haughty
features are unmistakably identifiable in the reclining head of
The Sleeping Muse, but not so with Margit Pogany, for here we are
confronted with a different approach. Little wonder that *Mlle Pogany*
became, in the good company of Marcel Duchamp, Brancusi's friend
and one-time dealer, a *succès de scandal* at the famous Armory Show
in New York in 1913, together with Duchamp's *Nude Descending a
Staircase*. But then, Brancusi's portrait is no likeness of the young
Hungarian sitter, as comparison with photographs of her reveal, any
more than Duchamp's image illustrates in any way the poem by Jules
Laforgue that inspired it. It has even been suggested that Brancusi
might have reacted to Margit Pogany's comment on seeing the
alabaster sculpture *Narcissus* as 'all eyes' on her first visit to Brancusi's
studio: 'I felt it was me'; and Brancusi, who was observing her, was

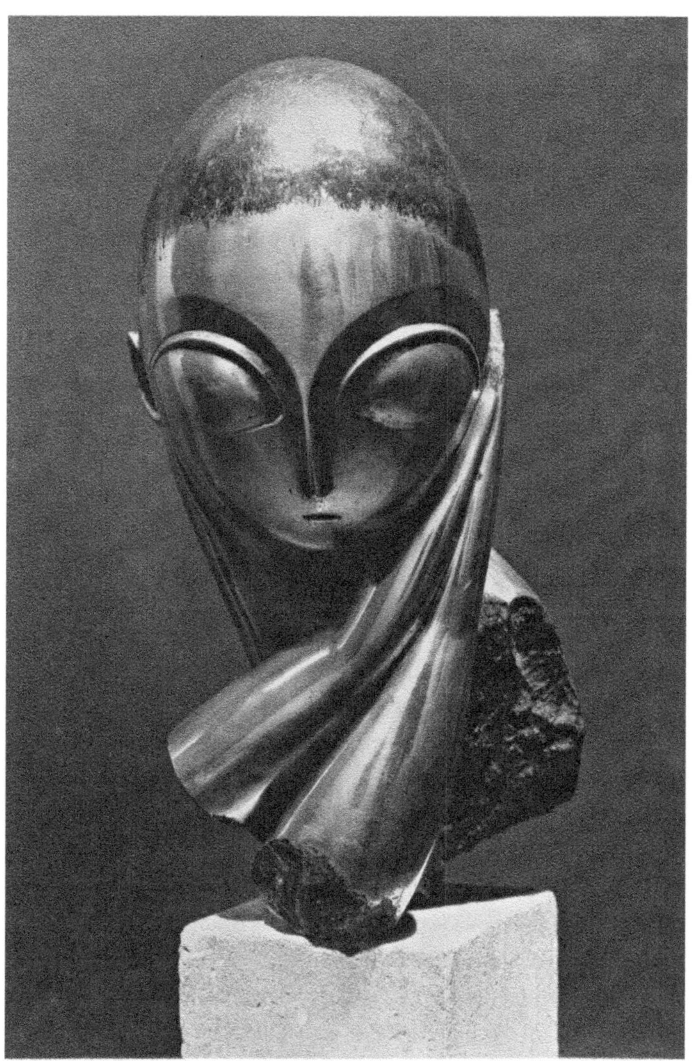

Mlle Pogany 1, 1913. The Hungarian painter Margit Pogany was Brancusi's most celebrated muse, and in this first version (followed by a second in 1919 and a third in 1931) we can chart the reductionist technique he was to employ in all his motifs.

'awfully pleased that I recognized myself'. Consequently he produced a portrait that certainly resembled the mysterious alabaster head of *Narcissus*, since lost,[37] rather than Pogany herself.[38]

Brancusi sent five works to the Armory Show of 1913 in New York: a plaster version (now lost) of *Mlle Pogany, The Sleeping Muse I, A Muse, The Kiss*, and a marble entitled *Torso of a Young Girl*.[39] The journalist and editor of *Vogue*, Frank Crowninshield, in an article, 'The Scandalous Armory Show of 1913', published in *Vogue* in 1940, analysed with hindsight that memorable event when hundreds of thousands of 'bewildered and divisive New Yorkers' had a first glimpse of paintings by Cézanne, Toulouse-Lautrec, Seurat, Van Gogh and Henri Rousseau, as well as sculptures by Brancusi, Archipenko, Lehmbruck, Bourdelle and Maillol. After New York the exhibition travelled to Chicago, where it ran into just as much scorn as well as 'charges of insanity and charlatanism'. Finally, the touring exhibition 'met its demise in Boston, where perhaps because of the congenial reserve of Boston's old families it awakened little interest, save from a socially prominent neurologist, who pronounced Matisse and Picasso to be victims of paranoia in its later and less curable stage'.[40]

It was the first, but certainly not the last, time Brancusi was to be ridiculed by press and public alike. In 1920 at the Salon des Indépendants in Paris, the portrait *Princess X* (a work now known to have been inspired by his sitter Marie Bonaparte) was ridiculed either by Matisse or Picasso (here accounts differ) one of whom allegedly shouted 'Voilà le phallus!', with the result that the sculpture had to be removed from the exhibition before the official opening.[41]

What links the 'scandalous' Armory Show with the later exhibition held at the Salon des Indépendants is that in each case we are dealing with portraits, specifically women's portraits. And Marie Bonaparte, the very wealthy great-grand-niece of the Emperor Napoleon I and wife to Prince George of Denmark, was one of the most shadowy presences in Brancusi's life. The sole piece of information about the

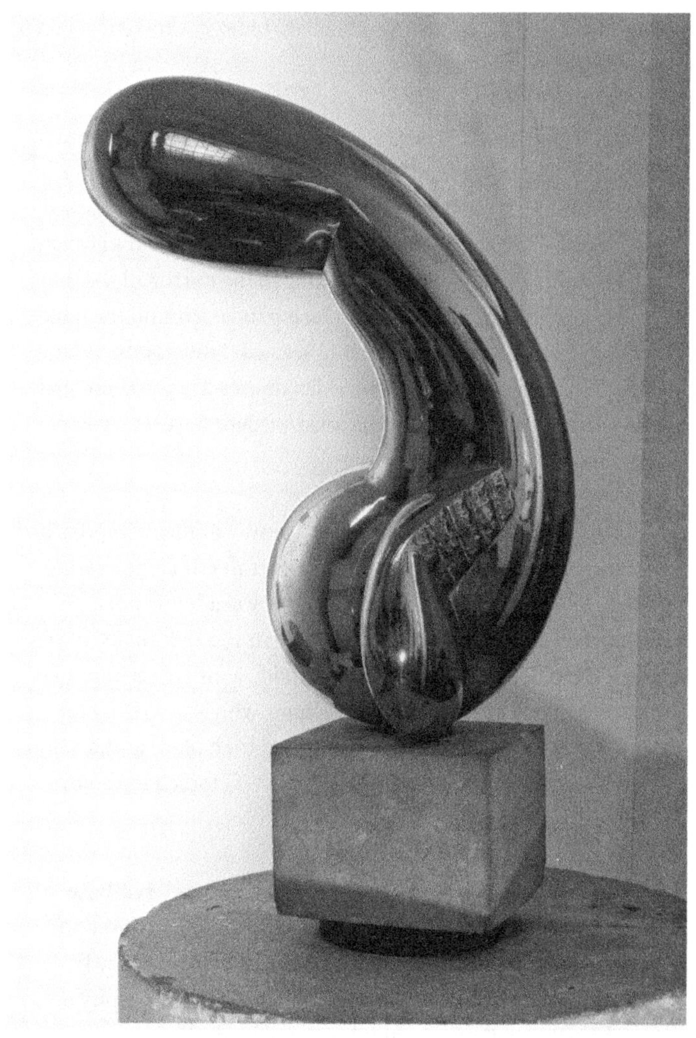

Princess X, 1915–16. The sitter was Princess Marie Bonaparte.

genesis of her portrait comes from Brancusi himself, who remembered her in most unflattering terms:

> A lady from Paris, a princess, insisted that I carved her bust. You know the horror and miserably low opinion I have about bust sculpture. She did not understand. She coquettishly asked me to make an exception. She had a beautiful bust but ugly legs and was terribly vain. She was looking in the mirror all the time, even during lunch . . . discreetly placing the mirror on the table looking furtively. She was vain and sensual. I did not intend to model the embodiment of her hidden desires. Do you think that this phenomenon happened unconsciously? I have a very low opinion of psychoanalysis.[42]

Both examples are also symptomatic of the way Brancusi approached portraiture, and specifically women's portraits. It is interesting to reflect that with the exception of the very academic portrait of his friend Ion Georgescu-Gorjan made in 1902, Brancusi never portrayed male friends. Brancusi also made a rather acrimonious comment to the journalist Roger Devigne, who was writing for *L'Ere Nouvelle* concerning the incident that took place at the Salon des Indépendants in 1920, when Brancusi was forced to remove *Princess X* from the show:

> My statue, you understand, is the woman; the very synthesis of the woman, it is the eternal feminine of Goethe reduced to its essence. . . . And I believe to have finally won a victory by overtaking the bounds of the material. Besides, what a pity it would be to spoil this beautiful material by digging into it little holes for eyes, hair, ears. And my material is so beautiful in its sinuous lines which shine like pure gold and which embody in a sole archetype all the feminine effigies on this earth.[43]

This significant statement goes a long way to explain Brancusi's approach to portrait sculpture with the important difference that by calling the work *Princess X* he deliberately obscured the sitter's identity. But for those who saw it, who was the mysterious princess? The end result was the refined final version of an earlier stone carving now lost entitled *Woman Combing her Hair* that Brancusi made in 1909, generally accepted to be the first stage of *Princess X* based on a statement by Nina Hamnett, who remembers seeing it in the studio:

> I had heard that he had done a statue of a princess. I had seen one that he did about 14 years before in marble, of a very beautiful woman with her head slightly leaning on one side and nude to the waist. He had worked and worked on it until it was almost abstract and resembled the same object that Gaudier-Brzeska's did of the head of Ezra Pound.[44]

In 1916 Brancusi sent two versions of *Princess X* (one marble, the other bronze) for exhibition at the Modern Gallery in New York, for which he titled them *Portrait de Madame P.D.K.*, a title that remains a mystery. It was the gallery's director, Marius de Zayas, who told John Quinn that Brancusi's sitter was in fact Marie Bonaparte. One year later the bronze version was exhibited at the Independent Exhibition in New York as 'Portrait de la Princesse Bonaparte'.[45] It is strange to reflect that when the portrait was shown in 1917 at the Society of Independent Artists exhibition in New York (10 April to 6 May), it was completely eclipsed by Marcel Duchamp's *Fountain*. This may well have been the reason why its unmistakable resemblance to a phallus passed unnoticed, but equally it is possible that the public was simply accepting it on its own grounds. Subsequently it was sold to John Quinn under its open title, *Portrait of Princess Bonaparte*.[46]

To what extent this work might have been an attempt at embodying the archetypal feminine is a question that is more easy to pose than to answer. His female sitters included Eileen Lane, Mme. Eugène Meyer Jr, Nancy Cunard and Léonie Ricou. Eileen Lane, a glamorous Irish-American with whom Brancusi had a baffling relationship, refused to recognize herself in the upright egg stood on its narrow end, topped by a comical protuberance. Eugène Mayer became an erect phallus, the only consession to portraiture as it is traditionally understood being the work's division into three discrete entities, which, with a great deal of good will can be read as Mayer's head, neck and upper torso. Nancy Cunard was portrayed as an upright half-ovoid resting on one leg and topped by a twisted curlicue attached to the tip of the ovoid, perhaps suggestive of her notoriously precarious life. But the most interesting portrait is the wooden totem with a pan and topped by a tuft, a work purporting to be the beautiful Léonie Ricou.[47]

For Brancusi, as for Picasso with *Les Demoiselles d'Avignon*, the year 1907 was that of the most radical technical and stylistic volte-face in his career. Leaving behind the Rodinesque phase that informed *The Prayer*, the influence of Cézanne notwithstanding, Brancusi embarked on the revolutionary technique of 'direct carving' with the series entitled *The Kiss*. This series would have disturbed his friends had he shown it to any of them, but he chose not to. An inexplicable silence surrounds both the circumstances of execution as well as the chronological sequence of the series. Between 1907 (the date generally accepted for the version in the Museum of Craiova) and 1945, Brancusi carved at least eight versions of *The Kiss*.[48] Among them is the only full-length version, which may well have been his first, although it is unanimously dated 1908, one year after the Craiova work.[49] Nothing is known about the circumstances of execution of the full-length version either, apart from the fact that in December 1911 it was placed on the grave of the young Russian student Tanya Rachewskaia, who had committed suicide because of unrequited love. Her fiancé, the Romanian doctor Solomon Marbais, purchased the sculpture directly from Brancusi to place at her grave.[50]

Unlike Matisse, Derain, Vlaminck or Picasso, all of whom were
proudly competing for the honour of being the first to have
'discovered' African art, Brancusi was so secretive about his own
experiments that we remain ignorant about them. It was Daniel-
Henri Kahnweiler who grandly proclaimed 1907 as the moment
when the avant-garde artists 'discovered' tribal art: 'In about 1907
several painters and their friends nurtured themselves with collecting
higgledy-piggledy sculptures from Black Africa and Oceania.'[51]
Things were quite a lot more complicated than this of course, as
Jean Laude revealed in *La Peinture française (1905–1914) et 'l'art nègre'*
in 1968, but ultimately it is less important to establish whether it was
Vlaminck, Derain, Matisse or Picasso who purchased the first tribal
artefact. What matters is that a series of circumstances 'have been
created which resulted in this African "discovery" and this "African
discovery" reached the ateliers very fast'. Simultaneously, 'several
painters discovered "les negres"', although each of them believed his
experience to be unique'.[52]

Between 1907 and 1908 while he was working on the first versions
of *The Kiss*, Brancusi also carved a series of mask-like heads (now
known only from photographs). The most important one is *The Head
of a Girl*; its photograph was published in 1925 in the supplement of
the magazine *This Quarter* dedicated to Brancusi, with the caption
'Première pierre directe 190 ' (the last digit of the date is illegible).

Brancusi continued to be secretive concerning his experimental
direct carving, and for that reason nothing is known about the genesis
of a crouching female figure mysteriously entitled *The Wisdom of the
Earth*, dated sometime between 1907 and 1908. In 1910 it was exhibited
for the first time in Bucharest at the exhibition organized by Tinerimea
Artistica, where it attracted the admiration and contempt of the press
in equal measure. Among those who were not impressed was his
former professor of aesthetics at the Academy of Fine Arts, Alexandru
Tzigara-Samurcaş. The work was subsequently purchased by the
engineer Gheorghe Romaşcu, and in a letter written by Brancusi

to his friend the painter Gheorghe Petraşcu, who had approached
Brancusi in support of Romaşcu's offer to buy the sculpture, he stated
that he was happy for Romaşcu to own it – and could he be so kind
and have the money ready to send to him.[53]

The strangeness of *The Wisdom of the Earth* explains the unusual
attention accorded to it by the Romanian press in 1910,[54] while in
Paris – the milieu that provided the inspiration for its genesis – it
was unknown. Yet formal analysis might just reveal a hitherto un-
suspected source of inspiration for it, which informed also *The Kiss*:
Egyptian art. This is particularly evident in the bust-length version
of *The Kiss*, which has been compared at a formal level with André
Derain's *Crouching Figure*, which Brancusi almost certainly saw in
the autumn of 1907 when it was exhibited for the first time at the
inauguration of Daniel-Henri Kahnweiler's gallery. Unlike Derain,
Brancusi was not looking at African art for inspiration, but at *Egyptian*
art. Comparison with the Egyptian 'Cube Figures' dating from the
period of the Old Kingdom that filled the Louvre confirm this. It is
also evident in the rendering of the hair, pulled back and falling in
straight parallel striations like an Egyptian wig, a peculiarity evident
not only in *The Kiss* series but also in *The Wisdom of the Earth*.[55]

Evidence of Brancusi's interest in African art comes to the fore
quite a lot later, around 1913–14, which became influential when
he was embarking on a new stylistic phase in his artistic career. But
before analysing his wood sculptures, a word must be said about
Brancusi's love of the animal world, which appears to be an idio-
syncracy not shared with his peers, with the exception of Picasso,
albeit late in his career. Brancusi's *oeuvre* is filled with all sorts of birds
and animals: magical birds (*Maiastra*); little birds (*oiselets*), birds in
flight, fish, seals, penguins, earth-bound tortoises, flying tortoises,
cocks, and in one instance, an unidentified creature of the night: a
nocturnal beast, *La bête nocturne*. In the simple humped shape carved
in wood, Brancusi captured all the ethos and mystery of the solitary
creature of the night scurrying in search of nourishment and shelter.

The series of birds was of special significance to Brancusi because he produced such an impressive number of variations on the theme, although there seems to be some disagreement regarding the total number, which varies between 34 and 43.[56] More important, with the *Mlle Pogany* series and the ovoids, they provide a seminal example of how Brancusi employed reductionism.

The earliest comprise the *Măiastra*, of which there are seven versions dated between 1910 and 1913.[57] Although its genesis remains obscure, which explains why it provoked such an extensive hermeneutics, a link between the fabulous bird from Romanian fairy tales as a source of inspiration and Brancusi's representation could be made. This may also explain his insistence in preserving the Romanian word ('*Măiastra*') in the title.[58] The description of *Măiastra* as 'the fabulous bird that leads the wandering lover to his beloved' by Brancusi's friend Carola Giedion-Welcker, which could in fact have been Brancusi's own explanation, throws some light on its origins. This is further corroborated by the fact that she goes on to discuss Brancusi's attempt to incorporate the abstract concept of flight in the subsequent versions entitled *The Bird in Space* by quoting him as saying 'All my life I have been seeking to capture the essence of flight'.[59]

The second more streamlined version, *The Golden Bird*, of which there are three versions, constitutes the transition between *Măiastra*, still unmistakably a bird with an elongated neck finished with a small head and a beak and a fat belly resting on the tripod formed by legs and tail, to the simplified *Golden Bird*, where the head and beak disappear and we are left with an upright neck flash with its thinned body while the legs and tail have been merged with the body. From *The Golden Bird* to the fusiform shape of *The Bird in Space* there was but one step Brancusi took, and achieved, as he confessed to Giedion-Welcker, his aim, but with preposterous consequences, for again Brancusi was lampooned for his radical art, this time in the form of a fine imposed by u.s. Customs. This occurred in 1926, when he was

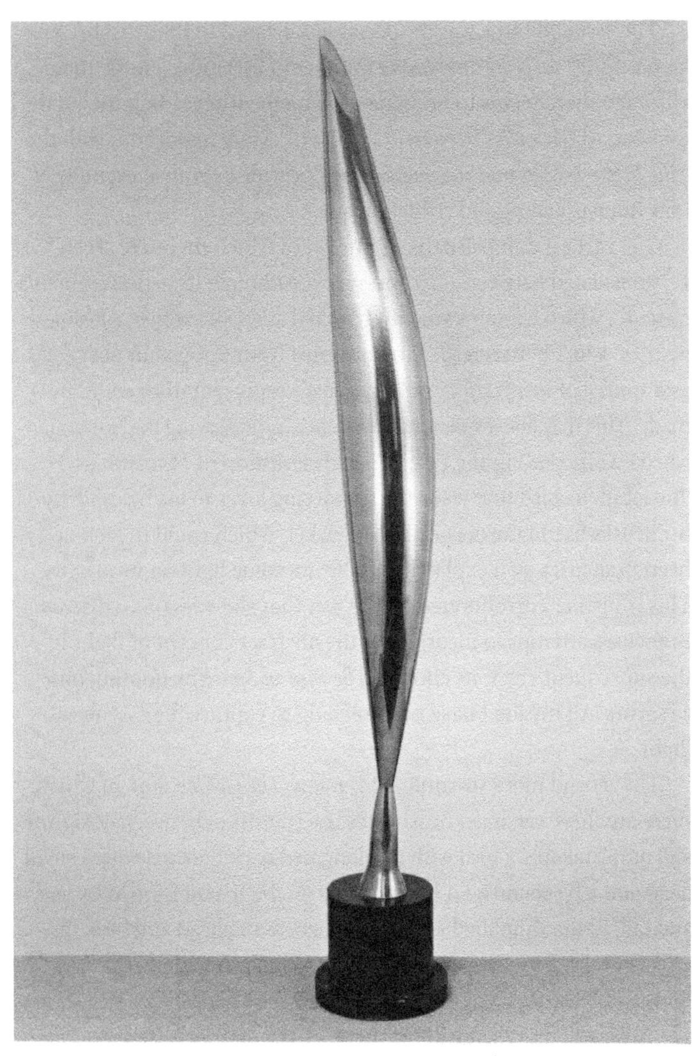

Bird in Space, 1923–4. Around 1910–12 Brancusi embarked on the birds, one of his most important series of motifs.

transporting sculptures to be exhibited at the Brummer Gallery in New York. The Customs put a levy tax of $250 on a bronze version of the *Bird in Space*, which the authorities deemed to be a 'utilitarian implement', not art. Brancusi went to court and subsequently won a well-publicized trial that became a symbol of Modernism's victory over petty philistinism.

Although Brancusi's personal life was ascetic and his work ethic rigorous, nevertheless he enjoyed socializing with Paris's artists and others, as Henri de Waroquier recalled:

> When I met him at the Rotonde around 1910 I realized after a few hours that I was dealing with a real man. He was passionately fond of life, more so than any other modern artist. He had a sense of the universality of life. When I knew him he lived at 54, rue du Montparnasse. He came to the Rotonde almost every day to meet Max Jacob, André Salmon, Gonzalez the sculptor, Picasso, Derain, Soutine, Modigliani, Delaunay, Blaise Cendrars and other artists and writers.[60]

Among them Henri ('Le Douanier') Rousseau and Amedeo Modigliani became close friends, as Brancusi remembered: 'I made friends with Matisse, Erik Satie, with Modigliani and especially with Guillaume Apollinaire whose death was a disaster for modern art. He was a superb comrade.'[61] But we find very little about Brancusi in Apollinaire's own writings. One of them however is worth mentioning here because it reveals the ludic aspect of bohemia that contributed to its notoriety, specifically targeting impasse Ronsin before Brancusi became one of its inhabitants. In an article entitled 'The Russian Painters in the Impasse Ronsin – the Truth About a Notorious Murder Trial: the Steinheil Case' dated 31 October 1910 and written for *L'Intransigent*, Apollinaire wrote about a famous murder mystery. The sole explanation of his coverage of this bizarre case was that it implicated in the

most inexplicable way the Fauve artists: Marguerite Steinheil was
accused of killing her mother and husband, the painter Adolphe
Steinheil, in their villa in impasse Ronsin on the night of 30–31 May
1908. At her trial, which took place in November 1909, she pleaded
not guilty by saying that they had been killed by burglars wearing
Levitical Jews' costumes stolen from a Jewish theatre. Mme Steinheil
was acquitted, and at the time when Apollinaire was writing his article
the mystery was still unsolved.

> Who said that the Steinheil case was closed? . . . The Russian
> painters have just reopened it. I confess that the spectacle awaiting
> me in the Impasse Ronsin was enough to impress the most cool-
> headed man. In the courtyard of the famous and sinister vial,
> I saw a group of persons – Russian or Polish Jews no doubt,
> prowling about, dressed in Levitical gowns. As I approached
> them and saw their faces, I suddenly realized the truth about the
> Steinheil case. What looked like a group of Ukrainian Jews was in
> fact a troupe of French painters among whom I recognized (I name
> them in the order in which I recall them) M. Henri Matisse, M.
> Othon Friesz, Mlle Marie Laurencin, M. van Dongen, M. Alcide
> le Beau. Also among them was a sculptor: M. Bourdelle.[62]

The reason for their presence, Apollinaire states, was this:

> These unusual assassins have come to exhibit their paintings in
> the very studio where M. Steinheil painted his. And to carry to its
> logical conclusion the fantasy that made them choose as disguises
> the costumes of the Polish ghettoes, our painters invited some
> Russian and Polish artists to join them in exhibiting their works.[63]

The macabre charade of this group exhibition notwithstanding,
it is worth noting that among the guests was Nadelman, whose work
Apollinaire praised:

The sculptor Elie Nadelman is exhibiting some drawings in which
the charm of perfect execution is joined to a noble and graceful
style that justifies the pretensions of an artist who is as yet too
unknown to maintain that he is continuing in the tradition of
the great sculptures of Greece.[64]

Nadelman (1882–1946) was a Polish Jew, which no doubt was
a contributing factor to the mischievous invitation of the Fauve
contingent to exhibit with them at the Steinheil Villa in impasse
Ronsin. Like Picasso and Brancusi, Nadelman arrived in Paris in
1904 from his native country. His first important Paris exhibition
took place in April 1909 at Galerie Druet, where he showed 'at
least 35 or 36 sculptures (13 heads and the rest nudes) at least
26 drawings and at least five relief plaquettes can be seen in three
general views of the exhibition'.[65] Their impact on the young artists
of Paris was overwhelming. Joseph Brummer, Brancusi's future
dealer in New York, at that time studying in Paris with Rodin,
told Philip Goodwin, the architect of MoMA, that Matisse 'briefly
maintaining an atelier on the *boulevard d'Orleans* where he taught',
posted a sign on the wall: 'Défense de parler de Nadelman ici.'[66]
Five years later Nadelman published in Paris a portfolio containing about 50 facsimiles of his drawings entitled *Vers l'unité
plastique*, which was re-issued in 1921 under the revised title *Vers
la beauté plastique*. In the portfolio, Nadelman, already aware
that he was not sufficiently recognized on the Paris art scene,
wrote that

These drawings made sixteen years ago (ca. 1905) have completely revolutionized the art of our time. They introduced
into painting and scupture abstract form until then wholly
lacking. Cubism was only an imitation of the abstract forms
of these drawings and did not attain then plastic significance.[67]

The complex principles involved were embodied in a plaster head (lost or destroyed) visible in a photograph taken of the Druet exhibition that Picasso saw in Nadelman's studio, and its impact is certainly visible in Picasso's sculpture *Head of Fernande* of 1909.[68] In fact in her book published in 1933 under the title *Picasso et ses amis*, Fernande Olivier singled out as an important new friend of Picasso's 'the very talented Polish sculptor called Elie Nadelman, whose works now joined the Steins's already abundant collection'.[69]

Both Nadelman and Amedeo Modigliani (1884–1920) were important influences on Brancusi's development during the crucial years 1909–1914, and in the case of the latter a close friendship developed that lasted until Modigliani's untimely death at the age of 36. A new artistic confluence between the three of them can be seen to emerge in 1909, but it was Brancusi who was the prime mover among the three. It was under the influence of Brancusi that Modigliani decided to embark on sculpture, and between 1909 and 1915 he produced a number of works. Twenty-five have been identified, but they may constitute only 'a fraction of his output'.[70] André Salmon recalled Modigliani's repeated visits to Brancusi's studio:

> To Brancusi's studio on Rue Vaugirard . . . Modigliani came and went, his hands in the pockets of his everlasting velvet suit, clutching to his hip the ever present drawing pad bound in celestial blue . . . Brancusi gave no advice, gave no lessons. But from there, Modigliani took the idea of geometry in space, different from that which was usually taught, on which at that time could have been found in modern studios. Tempted by sculpture, he tried his hand, but retained from those days in Brancusi's studio only that lengthening of the human figure, which characterizes so directly the style of his painted figures.[71]

The most revealing account comes from the critic Adolphe Basler, who mentions the impact of Nadelman rather than Brancusi on Modigliani:

Modigliani seemed to abandon painting [in 1909]. Negro sculpture
haunted him and the art of Picasso tormented him. This was the
time when the Polish sculptor Nadelman exhibited his works at
the Druet Gallery. The Natanson brothers, former editors of the
Revue Blanche, drew the attention of Gide and [Octave] Mirabeau
to this new talent. The experiments of Nadelman also disturbed
Picasso. In fact, the principles of spherical decompositon in
Nadelman's drawings and sculptures preceded the subsequent
experiments of the cubist Picasso. The sculptures of Nadelman
which astonished Modigliani were a stimulus to him. His curi-
osity turned to the forms created by the archaic Greeks, and to
Indo-Chinese [Khmer] sculpture that was beginning to be known
among the painters and sculptors and he assimilated much else
besides, though he always reserved his admiration for the
refined art of the Far East, and for the simplified proportions
of Negro sculpture.[72]

Modigliani's daughter Jeanne also dates the beginnings of
Modigliani's new career as a sculptor to 1909:

The discovery of African art about which Modigliani was
enthusiastically perorating, the examples of Brancusi, Lipchitz,
Nadelmann, Metchaninoff, have most certainly encouraged
Modigliani around 1909 to dedicate himself totally to sculpture:
but this was not in any way a sudden conversion. To become a
great sculptor was, as we all know, the great desire and fixed idea
of Amedeo and he never renounced it nor did he in fact give up
painting, during the period when he lived at Cité Falguière.[73]

Modigliani moved to Cité Falguière in 1909, His first-floor
studio was at 54 rue du Montparnasse, next door to Brancusi, and
he joined the new artists' groups that frequented the cafés of La
Rotonde, Le Dôme and La Closerie des Lilas. An equivalent of

Bâteau-Lavoir also existed with the ateliers of La Ruche, situated south of Montparnasse near the abattoir, which were inhabited mostly by those East European artists who became instrumental in the creation of the 'School of Paris':

Highly individual Eastern European artists lived there, mainly Ashkenazi Jews who spoke Yiddish, had experienced the ghetto and known persecutions and pogroms; for Soutine and Krémègne, who had lived through total misery and near starvation in Russia, the poverty at La Ruche felt like affluence in comparison. Chagall, who had lived there since 1910, was among the most eccentric inhabitants of La Ruche, with an extremely pale complexion and made-up eyes, he would paint dreams of Vitebsk and his fiancée Bella, at night, stark naked so as to preserve his one and only suit.[74]

Jacob Epstein arrived in Paris in 1912 to work on his commission for the Oscar Wilde tomb intended for Père-Lachaise cemetery. He described the charismatic Modigliani as 'short and handsome', but contrary to general perceptions, rather stocky. Epstein left a touching account of his visit to Modigliani's abject lodgings:

His studio at that time was a miserable hole within a courtyard, and here he lived and worked. It was then filled with nine or ten of those long heads which were suggested by African masks, and one figure. They were carved in stone; at night he would place candles on top of each one and the effect was that of a primitive temple. A legend of the quarter said that Modigliani, when under the influence of hashish, embraced these sculptures. Modigliani never seemed to want to sleep at night, and I recall that one night, when we left him very late, he came running down the passage after us, calling us to come back, very like a frightened child.[75]

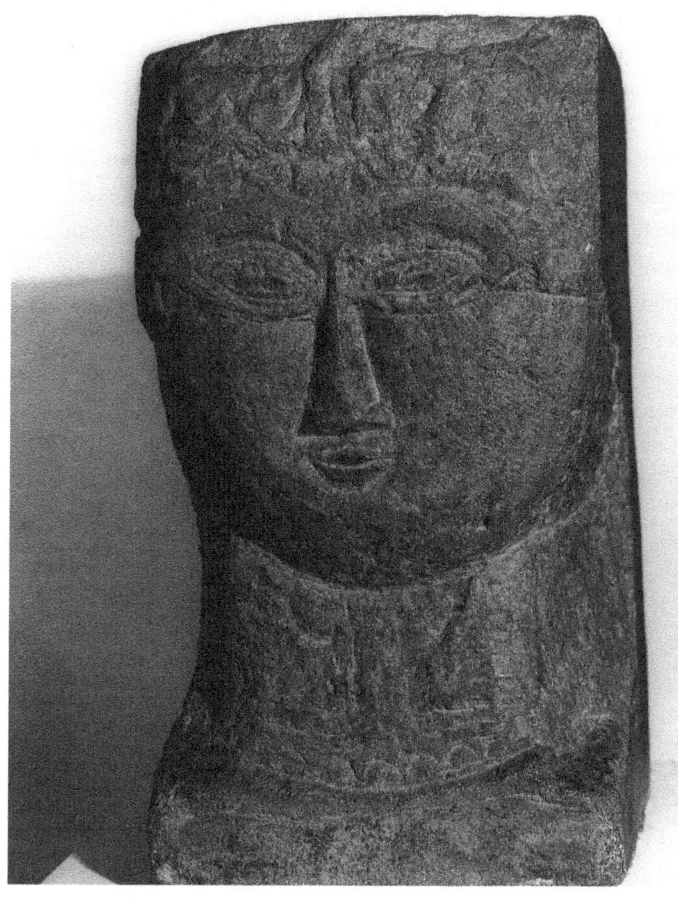

Amedeo Modigliani, *Head of a Woman*, 1912, stone.

Just as Modigliani was learning from Brancusi, Brancusi in turn was strongly inspired by Nadelman's experiments, whose influence becomes apparent in the series of ovoids.[76] The transition Brancusi made from the primitive vision that characterized his experiments with direct carving starting in 1907 and developed during 1908 and certainly into 1909 with *The Kiss* series, *The Ancient Figure* and *The Wisdom of the Earth* to the ovoids happened within the context of the portrait of Baroness Renée Frachon as well as – if we are to give credence to Margit Pogany's description of her sittings for the portrait – Pogany's portrait, where he performed his daring volte-face with the first version of *Mlle Pogany* and the better documented transition from the stone portrait of Renée Frachon to *The Sleeping Muse*.[77] Nowhere is Nadelman's influence more obvious than in the first version of *Mlle Pogany*, which can almost be seen as a practical demonstration of Nadelman's theories as summed up by André Gide, who attended the *vernissage* of Nadelman's exhibition at the Druet Gallery in April 1909 and noted in his diary:

> Nadelman draws with a compass and sculpts by assembling rhomboids. He has discovered that every curve of the human body is accompanied by a reciprocal curve which opposes it and corresponds to it. The harmony which results from these balancings smacks of the theorem. The most astonishing thing, however, is that he works from the living model.[78]

Whilst he was perfecting his reductionist technique with the ovoids, Brancusi embarked on another solitary journey, this time by turning his attention to a new material. In 1913 he produced his first work in wood: *The First Step*. Whether its title also reflects Brancusi's own tentative 'first steps' in using the new material remains a matter of debate, although this assumption has its own seductiveness. The fact that Brancusi himself destroyed it, save the head, after having it exhibited at the Alfred Stieglitz Photo Secession Gallery in New York in 1914 points to one thing: he must have been disappointed with the result. He did, however, put the wooden head to good use by casting several bronze versions of what was to become *The First Cry* after it.[79]

This period coincided with another important moment, this time not in his artistic career but in his personal life: he left his studio at 54 rue du Montparnasse and on the 1 January 1916 at the age of 42 years of age we find him at a new address: 8 impasse Ronsin, the forerunner of the studio complex at impasse Ronsin that will become Brancusi's *Gesamtkunstwerk*.

5

The Studios at impasse Ronsin

In 1916 Brancusi's new home and workshop at 8 impasse Ronsin
– a cul-de-sac off rue de Vaugirard – comprised a suite of three rooms
plus a fourth room on the first floor that could be reached by an
inner set of stairs.[1] At this point the idea of a studio complex in which
his life and work would become conflated in a *Gesamtkunstwerk* may
have started to materialize, but very likely not with all its subsequent
ramifications and functions. Brancusi was now moving from an
impoverished bohemia into a world of material affluence and success.
Although he continued to live and work at number 8 for over ten
years, a violent storm in July 1927 flooded his studio and forced him
to move across the alley into number 11. By the following January he
had established himself there for the long term, and soon began the
acquisition of neighbouring units: 'come and see my three shacks',
he told the editor of *The Little Review*, Margaret Anderson. (The
first ever article on Brancusi's sculpture had been published in this
magazine in 1921 by its then editor, Ezra Pound.) By 1941 his 'atelier'
comprised no less than five interconnecting studios, the fifth acquisition providing storage space for his plaster moulds and those works he
wanted to keep safe from prying eyes.[2] Thus, over the years Brancusi
was to live, work, entertain and display in an ever-expanding setting. It
was his wish to preserve this *Gesamtkunstwerk* for posterity unaltered,
and he was to make its preservation a condition in his will.

At the time when Brancusi moved to impasse Ronsin, he was
working with wood, his new material. Wood for him was a joyous

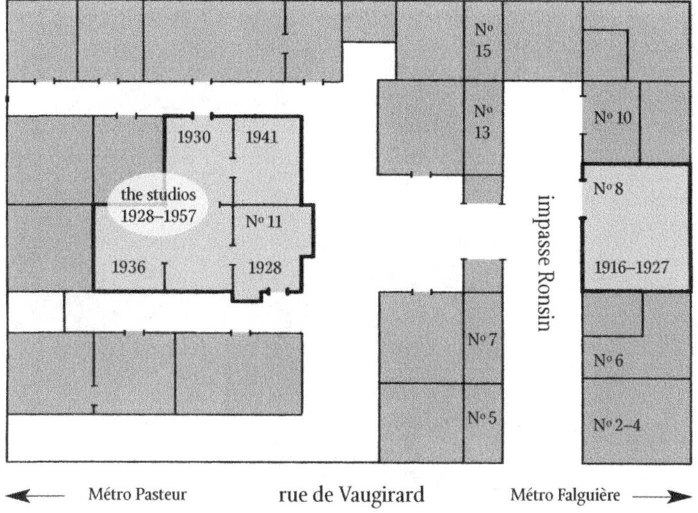

material, one that enabled him to recover aspects of his Romanian
heritage, but paradoxically he was also at his most experimental
with it, and that enabled him to introduce the intriguing practice
of using bases, furniture and sculpture interchangeably. Wood was
also put to practical use in the making of chairs, benches, stools and
bases, which in time were used interchangeably. Within the context
of these new categorical games we can align Brancusi's already well-
established practice of creating 'sculptural assemblages', whereby
several superimposed bases or bases supporting sculptures in
different materials, different colours and different textures would
switch function. One of the finest examples of this is the first version
of *The Măiastra* dated 1910, now in the Museum of Modern Art in
New York but formerly in the collection of John Quinn, who had
acquired it only with a wood base; its present three stone bases
were added at a later date. One of them has an additional identity
as an autonomous but completely undocumented sculpture, *The
Caryatids*. None of the three 'bases' of the present ensemble seem

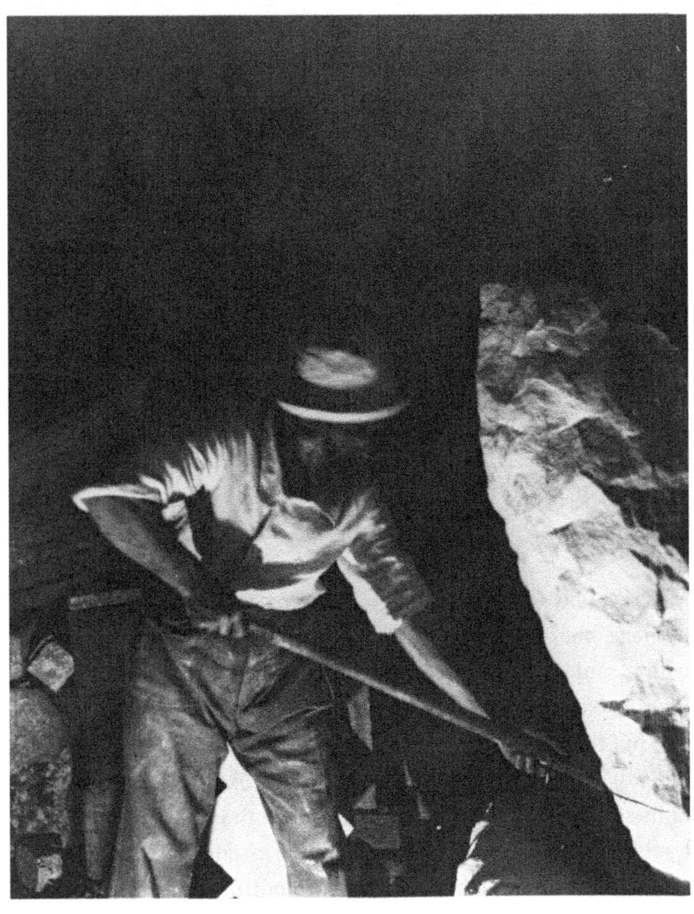

Brancusi at work at 8 impasse Ronsin in 1922.

ever to have been part of the Quinn collection.[3] It was given to MoMA in 1953 by Katherine S. Dreier.

There is little doubt that he was influenced in his experiments by his close friend Duchamp, inventor of the 'ready-mades'.[4] In later years Duchamp was to serve as Brancusi's agent, and he curated Brancusi's exhibitions at the Joseph Brummer gallery in New York

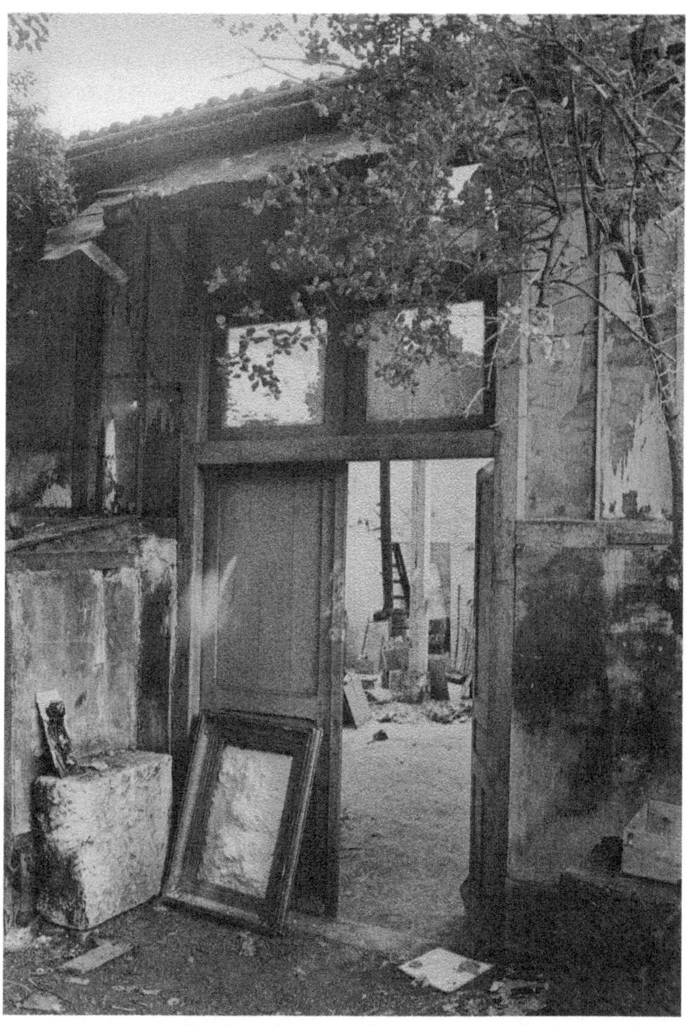

Brancusi's studio complex at impasse Ronsin, photographed in June 1961.

in 1926 and 1933. A comparison between Brancusi's handwritten list of works selected for the latter show with Duchamp's printed list in the catalogue reveals the extent to which Duchamp took liberties with the sculptor's own descriptions and choices of title. Thus the entry '*Pierre avec socle bois (trois pièces)*' in the handwritten list appears as '*Timidity*' in the catalogue. Perhaps more interesting is the metamorphosis of a mere base listed by Brancusi as '*Tabouret noyer*' into '*The Watchdog*'. Maybe Duchamp, as Brancusi's agent, was sometimes prompted by monetary considerations, for elevating the status of a mere base to that of an independent sculpture would have made it attractive to potential purchasers.[5]

The beginning of the friendship between Brancusi and Duchamp may go back to 1912, when Brancusi exhibited together *The Kiss*, *The Sleeping Muse* and *Prometheus* at the Salon des Indépendants; both Duchamp and Fernand Léger (who also became a close friend) were present at the show's preparatory *vernissage*. These three also had a shared interest in modern technology and its application in aviation, and together in 1912 they visited the Salon de la Locomotion Aérienne held at the Grand Palais, an occasion Léger never forgot:

Before the war of 1914, I went to the Salon de l'Aviation with Marcel Duchamp and Brancusi. Marcel, who was a dry sort of fellow with something of the ineffable about him, was walking among the engines and propellers without saying a word. And then suddenly he turned to Brancusi and said: 'Painting is finished; who could do better than this propeller? Tell me, can you make this?'[6]

The friendship that quickly developed between Brancusi and Duchamp is recorded in their letters, which were affectionately signed 'Maurice' or 'Morice'.[7] This was the pet name Brancusi reserved for very close friends, as Duchamp recalled:

Brancusi's intimate friends called each other Maurice. Not any old body could be Maurice. You had to be pure of heart to be a Maurice. I was very flattered when after two or three meetings Brancusi qualified me as a Maurice: 'You are alright. Altogether unsophisticated. Solid and good at everything, heart and intelligence. This is what matters for being yourself. Not more not less. Knowing how to pursue one's aims, be a free spirit, ignore doctrines, never to pontificate. Always to follow instinct and never reason. Yes, Yes, you can be a real Maurice.'[8]

Duchamp did not disappoint; he proved himself to be a firm ally. And Duchamp seems to have been instrumental in inspiring Brancusi's sophisticated categorical games with bases, furniture and sculpture. These permutations provided the conceptual basis on which Brancusi's studio complex began to develop into the *Gesamtkunstwerk* we know and whose genesis and stages of development can be charted from two primary sources: visitors' accounts and Brancusi's own photographs.

Brancusi was a passionate photographer and he took an astounding number of photographs of his own sculptures. The Brancusi archives contain 560 original negatives (the majority on glass plates) and 1,250 prints made by Brancusi from existing or lost negatives.[9] Significantly, some of the finest twentieth-century photographers, among them Edward Steichen and Alfred Stieglitz, became Brancusi's friends. And although he began using a camera as early as 1905,[10] Brancusi always wanted to acquire professional skills; eventually he turned to Man Ray for guidance. Their initial meeting took place at impasse Ronsin:

The first time I went to see the sculptor Brancusi in his studio, I was more impressed than in any cathedral. I was overwhelmed with its whiteness and lightness. . . . [It] was like entering another world – the whiteness, which, after all, is a synthesis of all the

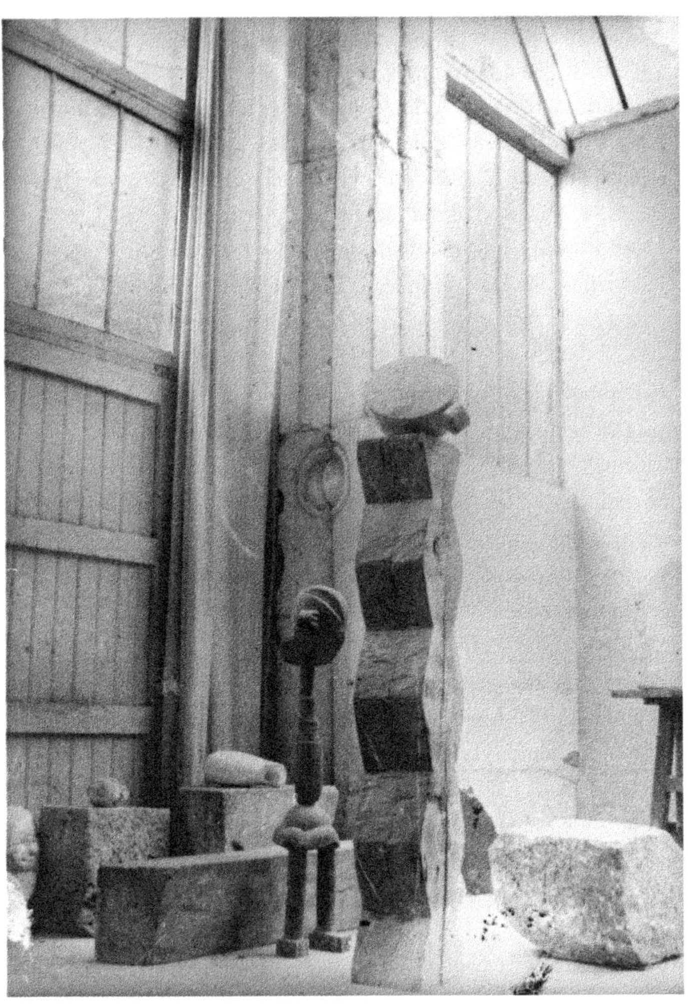

Brancusi's *The Child in the World*, 1917. Brancusi was in the habit of creating temporary assemblages, possibly for the purpose of photographing them and sending them to prospective collectors, in this case John Quinn.

colors of the spectrum, this whiteness extended to the home-built brick stove and long stovepipe – here and there emphasized by a rough-hewn piece of oak or the golden metallic gleam of a polished dynamic form on a pedestal. There was nothing in the studio that might have come out of a shop, no chairs or furniture. A solid white plaster cylinder six feet in diameter, cast on the floor of the studio, served as a table, with a couple of hollowed-out logs to sit on. A few small cushions thrown on these made the seats more inviting. Brancusi lived like a hermit, in his studio in the heart of Paris. Except for a few devoted friends, his work was practically unknown in Europe. He refused to exhibit – sculpture was the result of years of patient finishing . . .[11]

Man Ray does not give an exact date in the 1920s for this description of Brancusi's studio, though it is likely to be the earliest account of the emergence of the studio as a special locus for living, entertaining, doing business and making sculptures. He does, however, reference Edward Steichen, who is alleged to have convinced Brancusi to hold an exhibition at Stieglitz's Photo-Secession Gallery in New York, a show that was to take place in 1914 (12 March to 1 April). For the exhibition Brancusi selected eight works, and listed their prices: *The Sleeping Muse* (marble), *Mlle Pogany* (marble), *Danaide* (marble), *Danaide* (bronze), *The Sleeping Muse* (bronze), *The Golden Bird* (this was in fact a *Măiastra* and in the exhibition catalogue is correctly listed as *Paserca Măiastra*), *Naiade* (marble), and his first wood sculpture, initially titled *Premier pas*, which Brancusi crossed out and replaced with *L'Enfant prodigue* (this was also to be the title of a work made in 1915).[12] Man Ray got his information from what Brancusi had told him : 'This was not without its disillusionments, beginning with the customs which refused to regard the sculptures as works of art, insisting they were dutiable as industrial products.' There is no doubt that this part of Man Ray's commentary refers to an altogether different event. In 1926 'the American authorities imposed an import duty on the work [Brancusi's bronze *Bird in Space*], judging it to be a manufactured implement' rather than a work of art. The court case was described in detail in Jacob Epstein's autobiography; Epstein acted as a defence witness along with Steichen, the owner of the sculpture. After two years of litigation, a verdict in favour of *Bird in Space* was obtained.[13] We can only speculate that either Brancusi or Man Ray mistakenly conflated the two events; nevertheless it provides the *terminus post quem* for Man Ray's visit to the studio and Brancusi's 'professional training' to be a photographer, which happened sometime after 1926.

Initially Man Ray approached Brancusi with the idea of taking his portrait but Brancusi 'frowned; he said that he did not like to be photographed'. Instead he asked Man Ray to help him choose some photographic equipment and 'give him some points'.

The next day we went shopping, acquired a camera and a tripod. I suggested a photo-finisher who would do his dark room work, but this too, he wished to do himself. So he built a darkroom in a corner of the studio, all by himself, as he did everything else in the studio, even the moving of heavy pieces by crowbars and pulleys. Naturally, the outside of the darkroom was whitewashed so that it blended with the rest and became invisible. I directed him in taking of a picture and showed him how to finish it in the darkroom. From then on he worked by himself, not consulting me any further. Some time later he showed me his prints. They were out of focus, over or under exposed, scratched and spotty. This, he said, was how his work should be reproduced.[14]

Brancusi started to take photographs of the new studio at 8 impasse Ronsin immediately after he moved in, and they provide a comprehensive document of how it flourished into the most complex installation the sculptor ever created. What Brancusi created was a living, changing space visited by all sorts of people

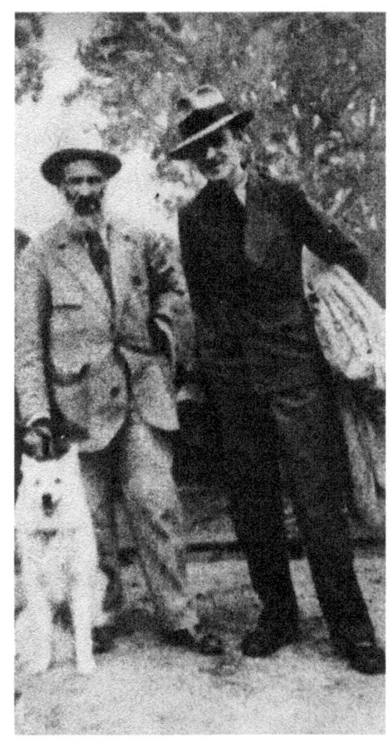

Brancusi, the Romanian Surrealist painter Victor Brauner and Brancusi's dog, Polaire, in 1931. Curiously, nothing is known about the relationship between Brauner and Brancusi, who met in Paris.

(friends, lovers, dealers, occasional others), filled with pots of plants, at one time home to a white dog called Polaire, its only permanent inhabitants being the artist and his sculptures. But even the sculptures were subjected to permutations and changes. The photographs document the gallery of people who passed through Brancusi's life and through the 'white atelier', bringing it alive, moments fortunately captured for posterity by a photograph or by a story.

The photographs also provide an invaluable means of documenting the subtle permutations continuously taking place among the works that brought the space alive; sculptures, bases, furniture would create a temporary *tableau vivant* only to be photographed and then dismantled and then reassembled in a variation on the same theme, or maybe into a completely different *tableau vivant* ready to be photographed again. Brancusi even had a name for these temporary assemblages: *groupe mobile.*

Thus in 1917 *L'Enfant au monde,* a *groupe mobile* consisting of a three-module wooden 'column' on which we can see chalk marks, topped by a wooden cup was joined by the second version of the charming wooden sculpture *The Little French Girl.* They were placed in each other's company very much like a family asked to pose for the camera to in order to provide a record for the family album. Was this an exercise in aesthetics on Brancusi's part? Or was there a more pragmatic motive behind them, such as a sales pitch? The latter hypothesis can be justified by the fact that a photograph was sent to Quinn with a customary accompanying letter dated 27 December 1917 in which Brancusi introduced the assemblage as *Bois, l'enfant au monde, groupe mobile.*[15]

Nor was this the first time that Brancusi used photographs as a promotional device. There is a series of postcards of photographs of his sculptures, all signed and dated in Brancusi's own handwriting, made between 1906 and 1907, at the time of Brancusi's artistic debut at the official *Salon.*[16]

The majority of the photographs Brancusi took, however, were targeted at the studio complex as *lebensraum* for its main protagonists, the sculptures themselves, although there were also exceptions. Thus in a photograph taken in 1922 we see his friend Léger dwarfed by colossal rocks and wooden beams thrown about that might have made the studio resemble the cave of a Cyclops were it not for a chair half-hidden from view, indicative of human scale and human presence. In the background the wonderful head of *Socrates* looms above the other wood sculptures, as if surveying the scene. In another photograph, dated 1930, we see Man Ray holding two batons possibly made of rolled paper, conducting, no doubt, an imaginary orchestra situated in our space, or perhaps the silent sculptures? The same arrangement of the sculptures provides the background for another photograph in which a bearded Brancusi attired in a white jacket

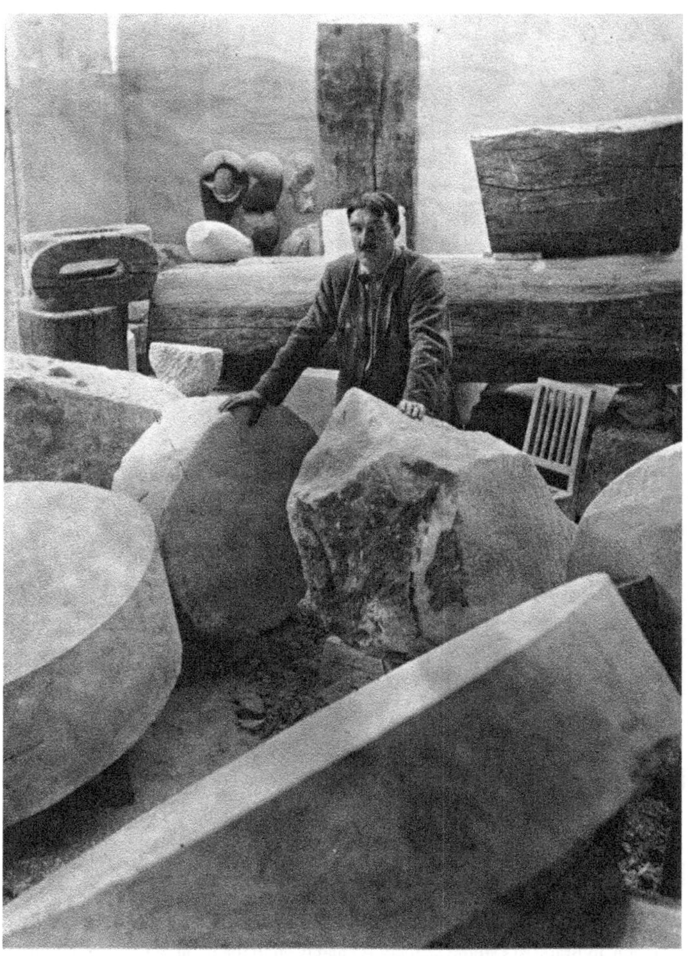

Fernand Léger in Brancusi's studio, *c.* 1922.

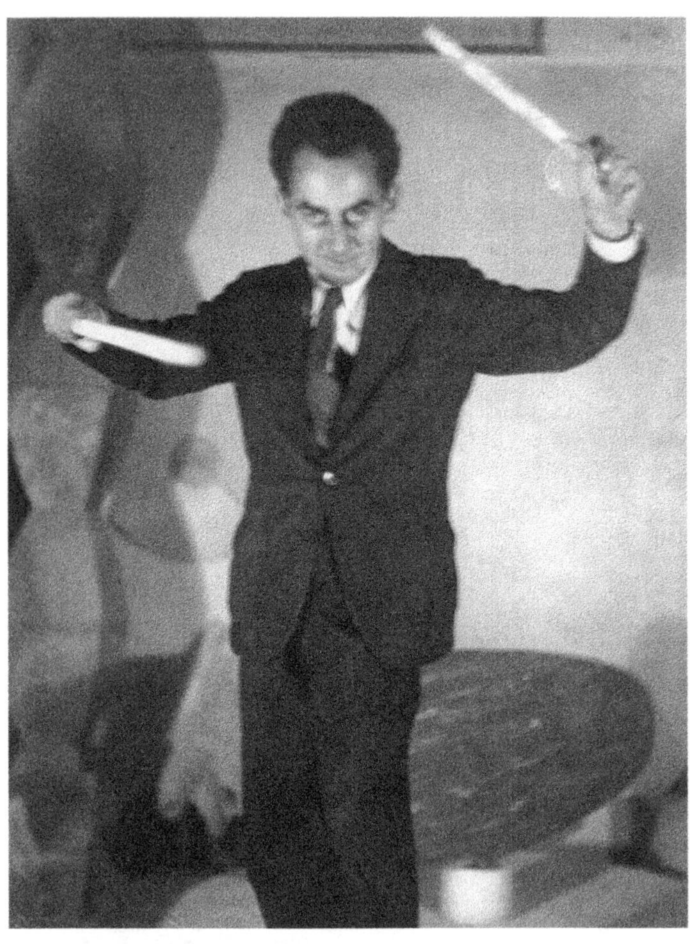

Man Ray in Brancusi's studio, *c.* 1930. He had been in the habit of photographing Brancusi's studios as well as individual works from the moment he arrived in Paris.

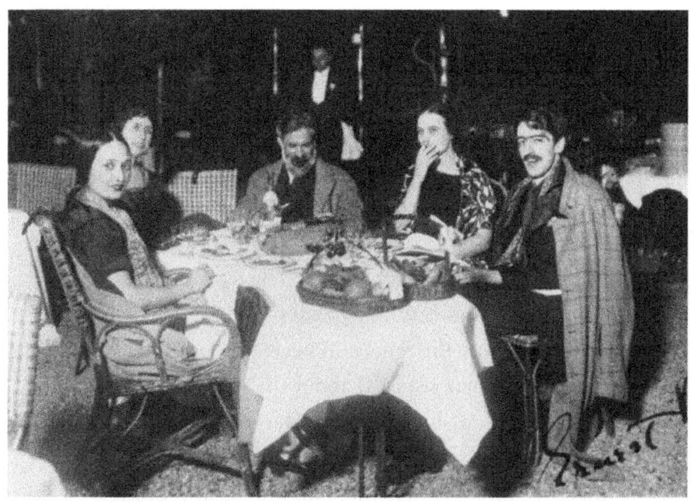

Brancusi and friends in 1925. From left to right: Lizica Codreanu, the British suffragette Ethel Moorhead, Brancusi, Irina Codreanu and the American poet Ernest Walsh. Moorhead and Walsh were directors of the arts review magazine *This Quarter*, first published in Paris in 1925. During the same year one of the supplements was dedicated to Brancusi.

and trousers is seen chatting up a young lady with bunched hair framing her beautiful face who wears a summery floral dress. Who is she? A lover? A collector? We simply do not know.[17]

Brancusi and friends! They bring his studios alive, although a leap of the imagination is required to create the narratives that fit these frozen images. It is, however, possible to get a richer understanding of how it really was from the written accounts left by Brancusi's visitors to his succession of white ateliers, the earliest of which goes back to 1906 when Brancusi was living at 16 place Dauphine. The psychologist and occasional journalist Dr Nicolae Vaschide (1874–1907), who was part of the wealthy diaspora of Romanians living in Paris (which included Brancusi's first collector and for a short time friend, Victor N. Popp), decided to take Brancusi under his wing by commissioning a portrait of his wife, Victoria, of which only a photograph survives. Writing for *L'Indépendance Roumaine* under the pseudonym Ion Magura, Vaschide was the first journalist to report back to Bucharest Brancusi's first successes on the Paris art scene. In one article he described the studio:

> I kept a touching memory of my last visit to his studio, a very small and modest room on the sixth floor in the place Dauphine . . . sketches, statues, ideas, projects, terracottas, fragments of happy attempts unfortunately left unfinished because of lack of funds before the cruel and necessary need to live. The cleanliness and beauty spread about the room, as well as the unshakeable faith he has in his talent, renders sympathetic not only the surroundings but also this man, who seems lost, overwhelmed by grand Parisian life. I do not know if Brancusi will become a great sculptor but at any case he is an artist motivated by the best possible intentions, in spite of the vicissitudes of a life of struggle and want.[18]

A visitor to Brancusi's later, more salubrious studio at 54 rue Montparnasse was Jacob Epstein:

> In 1912 I went also to the studio of Brancusi with Ortiz. Brancusi never went to the cafés. He was in the habit of keeping a number of bottles of milk 'maturing', and rows of these bottles were in the passage of his studio. He would exclaim against café life and say that one lost one's force there. No matter when one called on Brancusi, he was at work, and yet he always found time to be genial. He is, in his simplicity, truly saintly. He now drinks only hot water, of which he says 'It cures you of everything, even of love'.[19]

Brancusi's early studios conformed to the established norms of Paris-style bohemia as a space for living, loving and creating art where poverty and material want were compensated by youth, *joie de vivre* but also something considerably more precious: artistic creativity, as comparison with descriptions of other artists' studios reveals. Picasso's harsh beginnings in Paris certainly match Brancusi's, and this is testified by accounts left by Picasso's friends and by his first love and muse, Fernande Olivier. André Salmon, who had first met Picasso in 1903, left one of the earliest descriptions of Picasso's studio in the Bâteau-Lavoir:

> A painter's box on a wooden stand. A round table, small, bourgeois, found in the flea market; an old divan used as a bed, the easel. Contained within the primitive shape of the studio, a separate small room and inside it a sort of thing resembling a bed. It became a cubby-hole that the regulars called 'the room of the nanny'. All sorts of practical jokes took place here without the participation of the host, and this had been going on until the arrival soon enough, of Fernande Olivier.
>
> On the bourgeois table with Napoleon III mouldings, a petrol lamp was burning. There was no question of electricity, not even gas. The petrol lamp dispersed very little light. To paint or to display the canvases it was necessary to light a candle, that trembling candle which Picasso was holding high in front of me when he humanely introduced me to the superhuman world of his affairs, of his mothers without milk, the supra real world of *la misère bleue*.[20]

And this is what Fernande Olivier herself encountered on her first visit there in 1904:

> Huge unfinished canvases stood all over the studio and everything there suggested work; but, my God, what chaos! There was a mattress on four legs in the corner. A little iron stove, covered in rust; on top a yellow earthenware bowl for washing; beside on

a whitewood table was a towel and a minute stub of soap. In
another corner a pathetic little black-painted trunk made a pretty
uncomfortable seat. A cane chair, easels, canvases of every size
and tubes of paint were scattered all over the floor with rushes,
oil cans and a bowl for etching fluid. There were no curtains. In
the table drawer Picasso kept a pet white mouse which he tenderly
cared for and showed to everybody.[21]

Three years later, Picasso's new dealer, Daniel-Henri Kahnweiler,
made his first visit to Picasso's studio, and from his account not
much had changed. He told Gertrude Stein he would never forget

> Picasso answering the door barefoot, wearing nothing but a shirt
> and hastily pulling on a pair of trousers, nor the squalor of the
> downstairs studio: the strips of old wallpaper that had come
> away from the walls, mountains of ashes higher than the stove,
> the dusty stacks of canvases and 'the African sculptures of
> majestic severity'.[22]

Brancusi, like so many artists who arrived in Paris to forge new
lives and careers, was poor too, but here all similarities end. Unlike
some of his friends, who lived in utterly miserable circumstances, such
as his close friend Modigliani and the entire East European contingent
segregated at La Ruche, and to a certain extent even Picasso, there
was something luminous about Brancusi's surroundings, as Nicolae
Vaschide recalled, even the small studio on the first floor at place
Dauphine. By the time Man Ray visited Brancusi at impasse Ronsin
sometime after 1926, he singled out the whiteness of the 'cathedral
like' space of the studio as a moving experience. This may well have
something to do with Brancusi's belief that art and life were in-
separable; he would comment on the ancient Greeks attributing
the perfection, simplicity and purity of their art to the fact that it
was an expression of their way of life, and the white atelier was

without doubt the result of Brancusi's own philosophy influenced
by the classical antiquity. Nor was the metamorphosis of the early
studios – which were ordinary – into a studio qua *lebensraum* a leap
of faith; rather, it was a gradual process of gestation, as Brancusi
himelf confessed to Alexandre Istrati and Natalie Dumitresco,
who left us their testimony. Photographs of the early studios show
'sculptures higgledy-piggledy standing on banal pedestals next
to an insignificant chair of which Brancusi made a gouache and
showed it to us saying: "Here the last trace of a conventional piece
of furniture in my place."' By contrast the photographs of the
studio complex at impasse Ronsin show that a dramatic change
has occurred:

> the works are disposed in a joyous fashion, according to the
> taste of the *maître*, standing on robust socles. The plaster table
> destined for meals has the allure of a round sculpture, the bench
> which serves for the siestas is roughly hewn in wood, tabourets
> replace the chairs.

Brancusi altered even his way of dressing to fit his new environment.
He now sported 'white garments to work in, white hat to protect
himself against dust and marble splinters, sabots for his feet. . . .
Everything accords with a purer and easier mode of working.'[23]
It reveals also to what extent he was conflating his sculptures, his
life and ultimately himself into a total work of art.

Brancusi created his ultimate white atelier primarily in order for
it to function as a multipurpose space, firstly a living space for the
unfolding of his everyday existence with all that this entailed; second
it served as a workspace where he would patiently work on his
sculptures; and third (and perhaps more unusually) it also doubled
as a display case, a kind of personal museum and the *locus* where
sophisticated sales pitches were undertaken for prospective buyers.
Brancusi even acquired two electric motors that he fixed on the

socles of *Leda* and *The Seal*, which turned the bases and thus showed the sculptures in the round without his visitors being obliged to circumnavigate them.[24]

Brancusi, nevertheless, led a solitary life and for that reason the ludic dimension that coloured his social life was very important to him. This is particularly evident in his legendary generosity and love of entertaining and making merry. For the 1920s and even more so for the 1930s an impressive number of visitors have left accounts that tell us something about this secretive person who was Brancusi. One of the earliest comes from Jeanne Robert Foster, whom Brancusi invited to dine with him in 1922:

> A dinner cooked and served by him is an event. If two or three intimate friends have the rare privilege of dining with him, he will cook dinner over a fireplace of his own construction built into a corner of his studio. If one is a woman, he will set before her with a gallant gesture the handsomest plate in his cupboard, and arrange a bowl of flowers that drip the colouring of Matisse and Redon into the cool twilight. He is a connoisseur of wines and liquors and of strange fiery spirits, that, as one visitor said, would take the paint from the door – a mighty sculptor and a mighty wine.[25]

Less reverential but closer to reality is Nina Hamnett's mischievous report of her experience of dining *chez* Brancusi. The year was 1920:

> When one dined with him one had to eat and drink at the same time. He had marvellous burgundy and one started with some aperitifs. As the evening went on one got into almost a state of coma as the bifsteaks were certainly measured by metres, and the Pommard was rather potent.[26]

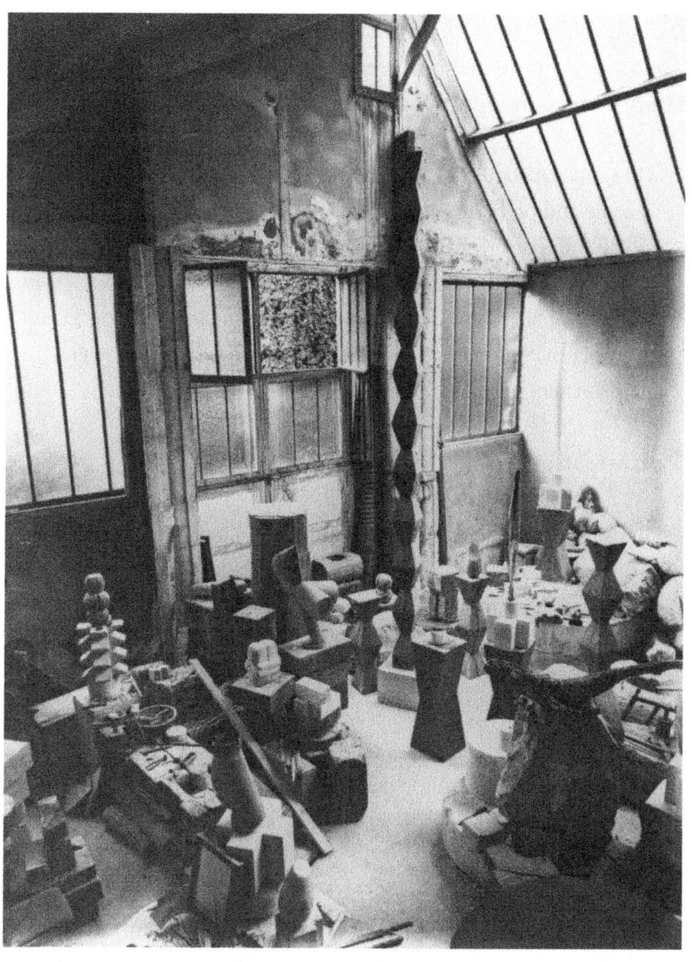

At impasse Ronsin in 1925, showing the *Column without End I* and *Crocodile* and other works. The *Crocodile* was a piece of driftwood Brancusi found on a beach.

Dorothy Adlow's record of her visit to impasse Ronsin in 1927 portrays
it as a 'lieu de presentation et d'exposition', which she described
rather masterfully:

One glances about the studio. There are many pieces of chiselled
marble and polished bronze that have been the subject of so much
ridicule and discussion. There is the portrait of a negress, a smooth
oval of marble with lips and hair, nothing else. There is a portrait
in wood of Socrates, an enormous skull with large, far-seeing eyes
gouged out. There is a torso that is little more than a triangle
with corners rounded. There is a curved column, a bird.[27]

Then her attention shifts to Brancusi himself:

In the midst of all of it stands that shy, anxious little gentleman,
Brancusi, revolving continuously the piece that one happens to
be looking at. He is clad in a suit that is as yellow as the sun, a
white canvas beach hat, and sabots. Those small shiny eyes betray
profound belief in whatever he chooses to do, despite the remarks
of the critics.

Suddenly Brancusi's cunning device of using an electric motor to
revolve his sculptures is brought alive, producing a magical effect
on his astonished visitor.

Brancusi suddenly said: 'You remember the story in mythology,
when a god was changed into a swan and Leda fell in love with
this bird?' His face had grown suddenly young and his eyes were
smiling like a mischievous child. He leaned over and plugged a
wire into a wall outlet. 'Well,' he whispered 'I never believed it.'
A strange brass form, poised on a revolving disk began to turn
around slowly, imperceptibly, before us, reflecting on its mirror-
like surface all the objects in the studio and ourselves in melting,

changing lights and shades. 'You see,' said Brancusi, 'I never
could imagine a male being turned into a swan, impossible, but
a woman, yes, quite easily. Can you recognize her in this bird?'
I looked more carefully as he drew his finger along the outline,
saying: 'She is kneeling, bent backwards. Can you see now?
These highlights were her breasts, her head . . . but they were
transformed into these bird forms. As they turn they are forever
transforming into new life, new rhythm . . . do you feel it?' The
luminous mythological bird kept on turning, its abstract surface
reflecting in silent, continuous motion the kaleidoscopic patterns
on the glossy surface of the metallic mirror below.

The magic of this experience is recaptured with *The Fish*, one of
Brancusi's favourite sculptures:

He lifted the dustcloth off the other work, revealing the glossy
veined surfaces of his great, flat marble fish poised on a single
pivoting point. Pushing this gently at one end, he said as it gained
momentum: 'When you see a fish, you do not think of its scales
do you? You think of its speed, its floating flashing body seen
through water . . . well I've tried to express just that. If I made
fins and eyes and scales, I would arrest its movement and hold
you by a pattern, or a shape of reality. I want just the flash of its
spirit. Do you understand me now?' I did.

Nowhere do we have such a clear explanation of the final purpose
behind the reductionist method that enabled Brancusi to penetrate
beyond the skin and bones in order to capture the Platonic essence
of his subject-matter, be it an animal, fish, bird, the human torso
or a portrait.

Two special presences in Brancusi's life were the art historian and
future Brancusi biographer Carola Giedion-Welcker (1893–1979),

whom he met in 1928, and Peggy Guggenheim (1898–1979). He first met Guggenheim in 1923 and then again in 1940, and on her own admission she knew Brancusi very well indeed: 'j'ai très intimement connu Brancusi'.[28] Both Guggenheim's and Giedion-Welcker's account reveal the differing aspects of Brancusi's relationships with women. A purely intellectual friendship linked Brancusi and the distinguished Swiss scholar Giedion-Welcker, who recalled the stories Brancusi had told her over the years, some of which she gave in one of the first biographies on Brancusi she published soon after his death.[29] She remembered that prior to her introduction she had anticipated a 'grand maître' who physically was similar to Rodin and who would receive her in a distant manner, but the contrary was the case. Brancusi was 'above all a subtle man, who welcomed me with a benevolence devoid of affectation whilst his malicious twinkling eyes were promising "fun for all".'

This is how he started to tell me a story about a costume ball where he disguised himself in 'beauté paysanne' and the hilarious consequences of his choice of disguise. During the course of our long friendship he told me a lot of other fascinating stories, some marvellous, some burlesque but always profoundly enlightened, at times by philosophy, of serene peace and interior calm, qualities this man has finally acquired but at the price of how many struggles, sufferings and experiences.[30]

If Giedion-Welcker was Brancusi's soul-mate, the rich and glamorous Peggy Guggenheim was many things in turn: friend, lover and eventually client. She recalled with admiration her first experience of the studio complex at impasse Ronsin in 1923, which she felt, was 'the place closest to Paradise on earth', ironically balancing that with the comment that Brancusi is but a 'semi-God' because, as she qualified,

He is also truly a man of this world, a cunning peasant; he loves
good food and he cooks admirably. He loves women but he
renounced all relations that might have threatened to interfere with
his work; he lives now alone, although he has a court of devoted
women, he treats like an old pasha. He has also a strong sense for
money. When he receives you in the atelier in impasse Ronsin, you
think that you are entering a sacred space, a Tibetan monastery even.
Brancusi paces quietly about the atelier removing the protective
covers from his sculptures and positioning them in the light that
shows them at their best. He would present them one after the
other during each visit as if you are seeing them for the first time.[31]

Brancusi and Guggenheim renewed their acquaintance during
World War II when she purchased two of his birds: bronze versions
of *The Măiastra* dated 1912 and *The Bird in Space*. She purchased
the former from Paul Poiret's sister, paying $1,000 dollars, and
charmingly described it as 'a beautiful bird with an enormous
stomach'. But she still 'hankered' (as she put it) after a *Bird in
Space* and eventually bought one from Brancusi himself in 1940,
just when Paris was being bombed by the Luftwaffe. She remembered vividly the occasion when she went to fetch the sculpture:

Brancusi polished all his sculptures by hand. I think that this is
the main reason they are so beautiful. The 'Bird in Space' was
to give him several weeks work. By the time he had finished the
Germans were near Paris, and I went to fetch it in my little car
to have it packed and shipped away. Tears were streaming down
Brancusi's face, and I was genuinely touched. I never knew why
he was so upset, but assumed it was because he was parting with
his favourite bird.[32]

One of Brancusi's last visitors was the young Polish sculptor Bohdan
Urbanowicz, who arrived at impasse Ronsin in December 1956:

It felt like you were immersed in an atmosphere of white and calm. A forest of sculptures – marble, wood, stone and bronze covered with mineral dust glistening in its whiteness. One after the other I find again the sculptures: the carved surface of a tree trunk shines like a rocket. A fish divides the space. The zigzags of a cock which crows. The *New Born* rotates slowly throwing lightning and reflexes as it does so. A poem without end of the wild silence, of the movement suppressed in silence. A roughly hewn wooden doorframe which recalls the gates of sub Carpathic silos was leading to Brancusi's room. And here we are again in an atmosphere dominated by white, reminiscent of a monk's cellar from Camaldoli. Above Brancusi's white head covered with a white bonnet the pale blue and gold of a small icon. A rough white woollen blanket, a few primitive stools, a few roughly carved trunks instead of a table, some tools thrown about. Brancusi was lying down, with his head resting on his hand. In his penetrating eyes you can notice the humour of an old man full of irony. He asked if we looked carefully at the sculptures. He only receives his friends, people who get pleasure from looking at his works, kind people and beautiful women, but not people who fancy themselves or art critics or dealers.[33]

A poignant remark Brancusi made to the young Polish artist – referring to the full-length version of *The Kiss* that became a memorial stone in Montparnasse cemetery – sums up what was the core of his belief and what he felt mattered most in life:

I received in Paris the commission for a funerary monument of a couple. Consecrating, as I always do, a long time to this sculpture, I realized to what extent the mirroring of the exterior shape of two beings is far removed from the essential truth. How remote are these sculptures from the great event of the birth of these beings, of their joys and tragedies, not to mention the grandeur of life and death. This is the story of *The Kiss,* placed in Montparnasse cemetery and composed in the shape of the letter 'M', *moartea* (in Romanian, *death*). . . . I wanted to capture not only the memory of this unique couple but of all the couples who loved each other on this earth before leaving it.[34]

6

Work and Friends

Qui est cette belle?
C'est Mademoiselle Pogany, une parente de Lady Shub-ad, la belle
    Sumérienne, et de Nefertiti.
Mademoiselle Pogany est la féerique grand'mère de la sculpture abstracte!

Who is that beauty?
That is Madamoiselle Pogany, the mother of Lady Shub-ad, the
    Beautiful Sumerian, and Nefertiti.
Madamoiselle Pogany is the fairy-tale grandmother of abstract
    sculpture!

These lines, written by Brancusi's friend, the Dadaist sculptor
Jean Arp,[1] reveal that Arp understood – as few others did – the
revolutionary nature of *Mlle Pogany*. Its first public exposure had
been at the New York Armory Show of 1913. Brancusi owed his
invitation to exhibit there to the American painter Walter Pach
(1883–1958), his neighbour in rue du Montparnasse, who became
one of the main organizers of the exhibition.[2] Pach was also the first
to 'discover' Brancusi's sculpture in 1910. Subsequently he became
instrumental in opening the lucrative American market to Brancusi,
whose reputation became established after the notoriety he achieved,
alongside Matisse and Duchamp, at the Armory Show. Pach also
became Bracusi's first important intermediary and dealer, succeeded
by Henri Pierre Roché (1879–1959), who facilitated and helped

Brancusi to sell his work to American collectors. Americans were the first to start collecting Brancusi's work, at a time when he was still virtually unknown in Paris. This explains not only the continuing admiration he enjoys in the USA but also why his finest masterpieces are in American rather than French museums. The extensive correspondence between Pach and Brancusi during 1912–25 reveals the mechanisms Pach employed in his capacity as the sculptor's self-styled dealer and public relations manager as well as the subtlety with which he performed his tasks.[3]

Notwithstanding the notoriety Brancusi had achieved at the Armory Show (although modest when compared with Duchamp's painting *Nude Descending a Staircase*, which became the butt of the sarcasm and anger of press and public alike), he was beginning to attract the interest of the collectors, and with none other than the much maligned *Mlle Pogany*. As noted earlier, in addition to a lost plaster version of this work, Brancusi sent four other sculptures to the Show, and in a photograph of the exhibition hall we can see them cluttered together on a high plinth in no particular arrangement.[4] They succeeded, however, in attracting some important collectors, with Arthur C. Davies, the Show's President, purchasing two marble heads, *The Muse* and *The Sleeping Muse*.

The correspondence between Brancusi and Pach also reveals the beginning of Brancusi's success with the American collectors. Thus in a letter dated 21 February 1913 Pach refers to 'your sculpture *Mlle Pogany*' and the fact that 'an enlightened amateur collector, himself a painter of great value' would like to own the marble version. Pach was cockily requesting Brancusi to quote a price, commenting that he had only supplied one for the plaster version exhibited at the Show. 'Could you please write me the price straight away and consider the sculpture as good as sold?' He also mentions that all expenses of shipping a marble version of *Mlle Pogany* to New York would also be paid for.

In his next letter dated 6 June 1913, Pach informs Brancusi that he has received a request for a bronze version of *Mlle Pogany*, and given that the plaster version was priced at 1,000 francs, he suggests double for the bronze. Pach mentions again the marble version, informing Brancusi that it did not sell but they would like to keep it for a little longer, 'nous réserver le marbre de cette sculpture encore' in case it will sell.[5] The interesting implication here is that Brancusi must have dispatched a marble version of *Mlle Pogany* immediately after Pach informed him of the 'enlightened' prospective buyer, who either changed his mind on seeing the work, or objected to its price.

Subsequent letters chart other interesting situations, including Brancusi's new friendship with Alfred Stieglitz. It is interesting that in a letter dated 6 February 1914 Pach advised Brancusi in no uncertain terms against doing business with the photographer:

Alfred Stieglitz is a rich, or relatively rich man who has this idea of being the protector of art in America. A good fellow, nonetheless he has no interest either in promoting the work of any artist or in paying any attention the rest of us who are staking our entire career for him and for this reason and also on their behalf we have decided to fight back as we did in fact last year. Frankly I think that you would make a terrible mistake if you were to send your marbles to his gallery.[6]

Brancusi of course would have none of it, as a letter sent a week later written in his terrible French reveals:

Comme je vous l'ai dit j'arive à me decider d'envoyer les marbres a New York. Meutenant elles sont en route et bien tot elle vont etre la bas. C'est a photo cesetion quelle don't etre exposée.

As I already told you I have now decided to send the marbles to New York. At present they are on their way and very soon they will be there. It is at photo secession [Photo-Secession, a Stieglitz gallery] where they have to be exhibited.

Pach continued to be peeved by Brancusi's relationship with Stieglitz, as his backhanded compliments regarding the latter's handling of Brancusi's first solo exhibition in New York reveal. In a letter dated 10 April 1914 Pach comments that the exhibition space is terribly small, rather like Kahnweiler's new gallery in Paris, and that the regulars of the gallery were commenting also that 'the exhibition at Stieglitz was very well organized regarding lighting and background wall colouring'. The shortcomings were that 'the exhibition space is very small (similar to that at the Kahnweiler gallery)' and that the visitors 'were chattering all the time, which did not allow for the calm required to study the works'. He then mentions that Arthur B. Davies bought *The Muse* and introduces a new client, a lawyer who is 'one of our finest collectors and a charming man'. He has already bought two works, a *Mlle Pogany* and *The Golden Bird* complete with base. This important new presence in Brancusi's life was John Quinn.[7]

Initially Pach acted as an intermediary between Brancusi and his distinguished new collector, but eventually Pach relinquished the role by putting them in touch directly. The extensive correspondence between Brancusi and Quinn, the first of which is dated 4 October 1916 and the last 16 February 1923, with the occasional letter written by Pach interspersed between them, provides an insight into Brancusi's own method of selling.[8]

To begin with, the letters reveal a formal relationship whereby they addressed each other as 'cher Monseur' and 'vous' and they continue to remain formal, although by 1923 'Cher Monsieur Brancusi' is replaced by the more intimate 'Mon cher Brancusi' and equally Brancusi to Quinn: 'Mon cher Quinn'. However, they continue to address each other with the formal *vous* instead of the more intimate *tu*. The subject-matter is strictly business, but in the last letter addressed by Quinn to Brancusi (16 February 1923), just before his untimely death one year later, Quinn talks for the first time about himself. Specifically he tells Brancusi about his terrible headaches, which prompted him to go to Hot Springs in Virginia, which did him good because by the end of the first week 'je pouvais dormir sans prendre des narcotiques'.[9]

John Quinn (1870–1924) was without doubt one of the major collectors of European avant-garde art. He started his collection in 1910 by offering Augustus John a £300 stipend in return for paintings to that amount, which Augustus John refused, recommending three younger British artists: Jacob Epstein, Wyndham Lewis and his own sister, Gwen John. The Armory Show opened Quinn's eyes to French art, and thus he started with Derain, the Duchamp brothers, Pascin and Segonzac, but not Brancusi.

It appears that Quinn's collection was never properly catalogued with the exception of the sole example published two years after his death, which listed 1,300 paintings and 75 sculptures, probably 'about half of the total of Quinn's possessions when the collection was intact and at its fullest'. By American standards Quinn was not even a 'typical American mass collector', but the reason the future MoMA director, Alfred Barr Jr, called Quinn 'the greatest American collector of art of his day' was precisely because Quinn did not aspire towards 'massive accumulation'. Quinn was a man who, 'in proportion of his means, garnered the greatest amount of excellence in such a way and at such a time as would do the most good to artists and to art'. Quinn had taste, 'but above all he had nerve and susceptibility'.[10]

The 1926 catalogue has a foreword by Forbes Watson,[11] in which he referred to the 'memorial exhibition of a portion of the collection of paintings and sculpture belonging to the late John Quinn held at the Art Centre New York in January 1926', which 'marked the closing of one of the most vivid and exciting epochs in the history of art in America'. On page 26 is a list of the 31 sculptures by Brancusi that Quinn had obtained over the years, among them five bases in wood and stone and one pencil drawing. Although judging by their preponderance, Quinn appears to have

preferred the smooth and elegant bronze and marble heads, he was
adventurous enough to buy the strange wood-carved *Chimera* as well
as the equally unconventional and overtly erotic *Adam and Eve*,
which unequivocally confirm Barr's characterization of Quinn as
a very brave collector.

Two other men played important parts in Brancusi's professional life: the writer Henri-Pierre Roché and his future dealer
Joseph Brummer. Henri-Pierre Roché (1879–1959) is less well known
through his association with the Paris avant-garde; rather, his reputation rests on his association with François Truffaut, who in 1962
made a film based on his novel *Jules et Jim*, written in 1953, when
Roché was 74 years old. During a visit to New York in 1916 Roché
met Quinn and became his 'scout', and Quinn was very influenced
in his subsequent choices by Roché's witty and descriptive telegrams.
Thus Roché became instrumental in helping him acquire in 1924,
shortly before his death, Henri (le Douanier) Rousseau's masterpiece
The Sleeping Gipsy, which he said, 'beats even the *Charmeuse*' (the
Snake Charmer). It was in fact Picasso who informed Roché that the
paintings were for sale and this is how Roché described the former
to his prospective client:

There is a desert, a distant range of mountains, the night sky,
a mighty strange stately lion against it; he quietly smells a big
sleeping woman, lying in the foreground, she is dreaming of
love, her face is INOUÏ, the lion is probably going to eat her, but
perhaps he will walk away. I have never been more thrilled by
a painting in my life.[12]

Roché's other new friend in New York was Duchamp, whose
notoriety acquired at the Armory Show pales in comparison with
what was to come later. Thus in May 1917 Duchamp showed at the
Indépendants an upended urinal with ' R. Mutt 1917' painted in
black on the rim: Roché was quick to join Duchamp in producing

the magazine they entitled *The Blind Man*, whose sole purpose was
to defend 'the artist' of the *Fountain*, 'Richard Mutt':

> Whether Mr Mutt with his own hands made the fountain or not
> has no importance. He CHOSE it. He took an ordinary article of life,
> placed it so that its useful significance disappeared under the new
> title and point of view, creating a new thought for that object.[13]

The correspondence between Roché and Brancusi covers a span
of 38 years (1917 to 1955); there are 59 letters in total, all of which,
with one exception, a letter written by Denise Roché, were written
by Henri-Pierre Roché to Brancusi.[14] The letters are very different in
kind from those by Quinn, and although business remains the prime
mover in their relationship, Roché also fulfilled the function of
an excellent public relations manager by bringing collectors to
Brancusi's studio with a view to encourage them to buy sculptures.

In the last letter published in the catalogue of the *Dation Brancusi
2001*, dated 16 August 1955, Roché refers to an important new project
for Brancusi, which unfortunately never materialized: the architect
Mies van der Rohe chose a *Bird in Space* to be placed in the piazzetta
of the Rockefeller Center he was in the process of completing, sug-
gesting a stainless steel version as his preferred material:

> The small space in front of the tower on the maquette is still not
> completed, we have just placed several trees around in order to
> create a green patch. Would it not be a good idea were you to choose
> the mode of placing the fountains, the water mirror and the shape
> of the fountain jets as well as the disposition of the green spaces.[15]

But collectors were not the only new faces:

> Dear Monsieur Brancusi: Marcel Duchamp passed me on your
> very kind invitation for Saturday evening which I accept with

great pleasure. Would you allow me to bring Erik Satie, who
wants to meet you, if he is still free that evening, which I am
not yet sure about.[16]

Thus through Roché, Brancusi was introduced to Satie. An affectionate and profound friendship bound Brancusi and Satie until
the latter's death in 1925. Although Satie visited Brancusi's studio
for the first time in 1917, their paths would have crossed before then.
Brancusi almost certainly attended Paul Fort's famous *reunions de
mardi* at the Closerie des Lilas restaurant in Montparnasse. These
events attracted Léger, Cendrars, Cocteau, Satie and later the short-
lived group of progressive composers who idolized Satie known as
Les Six: Honegger, Milhaud, Auric, Poulenc, Durey and Tailleferre.
Brancusi remembered one conversation with Satie that reveals how
his own intensity served to stiffen the composer's resolve:

The musician Erik Satie was part of our group. At some point he
was commissioned to write an opera. The group had to make it
to the Grand Opéra. At long last, Erik Satie, the favourite child of
the group received a well-paid opera commission. He was writing
without effort. Whilst I was engaged with my *Măiastra* he visited
my atelier. I was tired, disappointed and troubled. Erik Satie asked
what was the cause. I replied: 'Because I have to eliminate a shadow
from the neck of the *Măiastra*. It was important that a certain line
had to come out in relief. A billion lines pass through a point and
I have to choose from a billion lines, one, a single line.' Erik Satie
who was working on the opera which was commissioned from
him, dropped the commission and returned to his own music.
The other six musicians of his group made it to the Opera, but
it is not the same thing. Erik Satie cannot be imitated.[17]

Around 1917 the idea of setting Plato's *Dialogues* to music had
begun to materialize in Satie's mind, and two years later Princess

Edmund de Polignac commissioned him to set the event of Socrates' death to music. Its premiere took place on 14 February 1920 at a concert organized by the Société Nationale de Musique, but it was not a success: 'The audience, by this point expecting humour from Satie, profoundly misunderstood the work and laughed at the philosopher's death, whilst the critics responded with hostility'.[18] At the same time as Satie had begin work on *La Mort de Socrate*, Brancusi began on his sculpture *Socrates*, which he completed in 1922. He was deeply entrenched in this project, and it appears that he often discussed its progress with Satie.[19] It also seems likely that Satie discovered Romanian folk music through his friendship with Brancusi. The book on Satie published in Bucharest in 1945 that was written by Brancusi's Romanian friend V. G. Paleolog includes a chapter on the composer's links to Romanian music; Paleolog assumed that Satie would have heard Romanian music at the 1889 Universal Exhibition in Paris, at which Romania exhibited. Maybe so, but Paleolog failed to consider that Brancusi, whose prized collection of records shows his love of international folk music and who was himself a keen amateur violin player, would have played Romanian folk music to Satie. Nevertheless his conclusion regarding Romanian folk influences on Satie's music seem apposite: 'Without doubt the transparent sonorities which are at the forefront of Satie's music would have been suggested by the use of the panpipe designed with a very specific sonorous contour without shadows or enharmonic sounds.'[20]

Satie's death in 1925 was remembered by Brancusi in a sobering way:

When Satie died full of debts, a few of us who were his friends got together, paid his debts and took over the objects left in his apartment in order to avoid them being sold at public auction. It is a horrible thing of which I am afraid. Three years ago, when I was seriously ill, on my death bed, I almost died. In fact you

only die when you are taken by surprise or when you yourself
have decided to die. But at the very thought that my four ateliers,
filled with souvenirs, with finished and unfinished things could
be acquisitioned by the hyenas, I decided not to die anymore.
My doctor considered that I was lost. He decided to put me in
a hospice with the morgue and the cemetery nearby. I knew
what he was thinking. When he arrived the following morning
I declared jokingly: 'Doctor, I decided not to die anymore!'
And I am still alive.[21]

Another possible collaboration between Brancusi and Satie
involved costume design. Brancusi designed a stage costume for
the Romanian classical dancer Lizica Codreanu that may have been
intended for a performance of Satie's *Gymnopédies*, written many
years before, although there is no documentary evidence to that
effect. The Codreanu sisters, Irina and Lizica, were friends of Brancusi,
and Irina, who was training as a sculptor, became for a short time his
apprentice. As a rule, Brancusi did not approve of apprentices; Irina
Codreanu was his first exception. During one of her visits to the studio
in 1922, Brancusi joked that 'I would not dare touch beautiful girls
like you even with a flower.' In the end he relented and Irina, together
with another Romanian sculptor, Sanda Kessel, who at that time was
also working in Emile-Antoine Bourdelle's studio at the Académie de
la Grande Chaumière, started with Brancusi. In order to allow himself
to be severe with his new apprentices, he nicknamed Sanda Kessel
Petrica while Irina was *Costica*.

He taught us the technique of direct carving in stone and wood
and the technique of polishing bronze. But especially during
our dinner conversations – he loved cooking for friends and he
cooked very well – we were learning a lot. He was expressing his
ideas with the simplicity and plasticity of the countryman. He was
formulating them as axioms, coloured by his rich imagination,

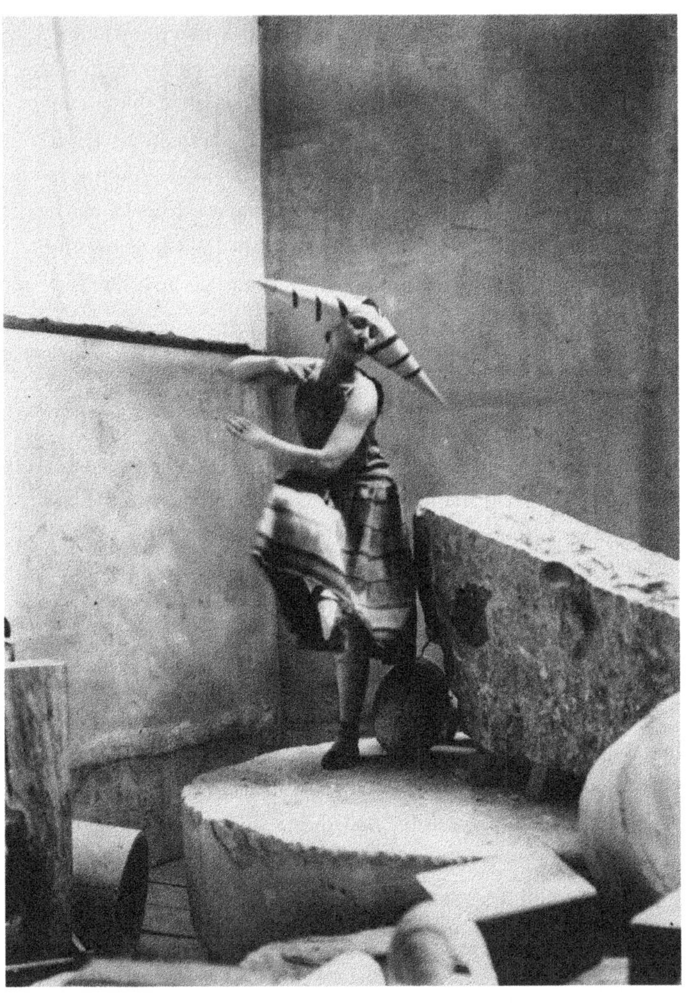

Lizica Codreanu in Brancusi's studio in 1922. Her dance costume was designed by Brancusi and possibly for the ballet *Gymnopédies*, with music by Erik Satie.

full of unexpected improvization. Brancusi gave us the true
sense of the block of stone, marble and the tree trunk. In other
words he taught us how to respect the shape which nature
or accident gave matter and start from this point to find the
adequate sculptural structure.[22]

Irina also remembers Brancusi playing Romanian folk tunes and
dances on the violin, often accompanied by his friend the Romanian
composer Mihai Mihailovici, while on other occasions 'he was
inventing dances . . . that underlined the graceful gestures and
curious rhythms of the illustrious dancer'.[23]

Two photographs of Lizica Codreanu in Brancusi's studio show
her wearing the costume designed for her but nothing seems to be
known about the circumstances of their creation or indeed whether
she performed in public in it.[24] We do know that she danced at the
famous *Soirée du Coeur à barbe* that took place on 6 July 1929 at Salle
du Théâtre Michel, when Tristan Tzara's *La Coeur à Gas* with cardboard costumes designed by Sonia Delaunay was also performed.
It was also on this occasion that 'a favourite poem added at the last
minute by Iliazde has added a little more substance to the piece
danced by Lizica Codreanu'. Might she have worn the costume
Brancusi designed for her at the Dada soirée? The occasion was
certainly appropriate for Brancusi's outrageous outfit, but there is
no mention of the music she danced to, which may well have been
written by Satie. Brancusi's costume was a dowdy dress complemented
by a ridiculous headdress consisting of a pair of conical witch-like
hats made of what looks like cardboard. In one of the photographs
the cone decorated with a simple black line drawn lengthwise is
placed on the dancer's head upright like a witch's hat whilst the second
is an even sillier headdress consisting of two cones decorated with
a spiralling stripe that jut outwards, covering the ears. They give
the dancer a clownish appearance that conflicts with her grave face
and hierarchic pose.[25]

Brancusi was never directly involved with Dadaism despite his friendship with Duchamp and Francis Picabia. Thus on 27 March 1920 he attended Breton's reading of Picabia's *Manifeste cannibale*, which was staged on 26 May at Salle Gaveau. The audience was treated to an outrageous Dadaist spectacle, which included Breton with a revolver attached to each temple, Eluard as a ballerina, Fraenkel in an apron, Soupault in shirtsleeves and all the other Dadaists wearing tubes or funnels on their heads. Breton started to read Picabia's *Manifeste cannibale*, was pelted with tomatoes by the public and all hell broke loose.[26] Brancusi was standing in the wings near a young woman who was supposed to go on stage naked and shout '*merde!*'; not surprisingly she was paralyzed by fear. Brancusi talked her into not dwelling too much on what she was expected to do but to do it anyway, and in the end all went well.[27]

Of course, one of the originators of the Dada movement in 1916 in Zürich was none other than Tristan Tzara (1896–1963), another Romanian. His real name was Samuel Rosenstock. He arrived in Zürich in 1915 and between that date and his departure for Paris in 1919 he became instrumental as one of the founders of Cabaret Voltaire, alongside an international constellation of disenchanted intellectuals and artists, including Hugo Ball and his mistress Emmy Hennings, Jean Arp, Marcel Janco and Richard Huelsenbeck. A fellow Dadaist remembered Tzara as a small but uninhibited man:

He was a David who knew how to hit every Goliath in exactly the right spot with a bit of stone, earth or manure, with or without the accompaniment of witty *bons-mots*, back-answers and sharp splinters of linguistic granite. Life and language were his chosen arts, and the wilder the surrounding fracas, the livelier he became. What Tzara did not know, could not do, would not dare to do, had not yet been thought of. His crafty grin was full of humour but also full of tricks; there was never a dull moment with him.[28]

Tzara's first visit to Brancusi's studio took place in 1921, following
a polite letter written on 12 July:

Dear friend, Mme Picabia, Man Ray, an American lady and
myself have the urge to come and see you tomorrow after dinner.
This is if it does not disturb you. I would be very pleased to see
you, let me know if this is inconvenient. In this case, let me know
c/o Librairie six (for Tzara).

Beneath the signature is a drawing of a flower, and beneath that 'les
yeux ouverts'.[29]

Two other Romanian poets became Brancusi's friends at about
the same time: Ilarie Voronca (1903–1948) and Benjamin Fondane
(1898–1944). In 1929 Voronca commissioned Brancusi to illustrate a
volume of his poems entitled *Plante si animale* (Plants and Animals),
which was published that same year in Paris. Brancusi made three pen
drawings for it. Delicate and playful, they reflect Brancusi's love for
the natural world: a somewhat bemused cow with its tail in a curlicue,
a snail, birds in flight reduced to hovering triangles requiring a leap
of the imagination to identify them, yet they are clearly not in any
way similar to the abstract Arp-like configurations of one of the
drawings.[30]

Brancusi also drew the portrait of the poet Benjamin Fondane.
Virtually unknown and still unrecognized, Fondane was a true
polymath – poet, essayist, filmmaker and director. He left Romania
in 1923 and settled in Paris, where his first job was that of private
librarian working for the brothers Remy and Jean de Gourmont
and lodging with them in their apartment in rue de Saint-Péres.
In 1928 Fondane's volume of poems, *Trois scenarios ciné-poèmes*,
with photographs by Man Ray, was published in Paris. Meanwhile
he was also writing quantities of essays, articles and features for a
variety of publications, in particular the prestigious *Cahiers du sud*.
Among them was an article entitled 'Brancusi', published in *Cahiers*

de l'étoile in 1929.[31] Later, during the Nazi occupation of Paris, Fondane, then in hiding, was eventually betrayed by the caretaker; he was deported in the last convoy that left Drancy for Auschwitz, where he died in 1944.[32]

Another long correspondence involving Brancusi is the one he enjoyed with the Romanian composer M. Mihalovici (1898–1985) between 1923 and 1955, although Mihalovici is barely mentioned in writings on Brancusi. The sculptor was particularly fond of popular entertainment, and would go to the Mille Colonnes cinema in Montparnasse to hear his friend playing the piano in accompaniment to silent films of that era:

> He liked to go to Bobino music hall or to the theatre de Montparnasse. The bedroom farces presented in these theatres amused him no end. He was especially fond of an actor called Montéus who would often interrupt his speeches to make cracks at the audience. He liked to applaud the bearded man with the soprano voice and together with his friends Soutine and Granovski would make such a racket that they were sometimes thrown out of the theatre. . . . He adored popular dance-halls, carnivals, roller-coasters and see-saws; they reminded him of the merry-making of his youth. He drank a great deal but never got drunk. When one of his friends was in his cups he would grab him by the scruff of his neck and spin him around like a top. This would sober up the friend sufficiently to go on enjoying the party.[33]

Brancusi's enthusiasm for disguise, dissimulation and role-playing testifies also to a lesser known Dionysian dimension of his character, in contrast with the Apollonian serenity of his sculptures, and his studio provided the perfect back-drop for his Homeric banquets and seductions of beautiful female visitors. Presenting his sculptures to prospective buyers or just to those visitors he felt would love them became a veritable spectacle, starting with the dramatic removal of the protective dust-cloths. He would find the most advantageous lighting for the display of his works, and as if this were not enough, they would also begin to rotate slowly, hypnotizing those looking on. Meanwhile he would explain their meaning to his captive audience or perhaps just tell a funny story.

The passion for disguise was not something Brancusi discovered in Paris; we find him in drag in Craiova when he was a mere teenager aged about 18, as a charming, if perhaps apocryphal, story reveals. Brancusi fell in love for the first time with a beautiful but poor girl, Ioana, whose mother Gheorghina was a washerwoman. The fashion for women at that time was to wear starched white petticoats and panties, with blouses gathered at the neck. On one occasion during the Jewish celebration of Purim, Constantin and Ioana exchanged clothes, she wearing his school uniform, he attired in her skirts and petticoats and with horsehair stuffed under the blouse to simulate breasts; the ensemble was completed by a wide-brimmed hat. Cross-dressed in this way, the pair wandered the streets of Craiova's Jewish ghetto. Nothing apart from a 'stolen kiss' happened between them, but it was a very special kiss, one that Brancusi later confessed 'I will never forget for as long as I live'.[34] If we can give credence to this charming story, then this is the earliest example that testifies to Brancusi's curious propensity for cross-dressing as well as dressing up. He was in fact acknowledged as a master of disguise.

His enthusiasm for merrymaking remained undiminished and Paris offered endless opportunities, especially during the *Années folles*, when every week there would be a costume ball or a special event organized by one or other of the countless societies and charities as well as wealthy socialites. Montparnasse was the premier venue for events such as these:

The most serious artists participated . . . one could see Gromaire dressed as a Spanish Jesuit wearing under his cassock frilly bloomers adorned with pink ribbons . . . and Brancusi: 'a genius of disguise dressed as a street singer or maybe as an oriental satrap. An old Persian carpet on his back and a necklace made of smalls bells gave a perfect illusion.'[35]

But what is one to make of the following anecdote? The year was 1922, as Nina Hamnett recalled:

I dined . . . at the Swedish Restaurant in Montparnasse and we went to the Rue Boisy d'Anglais about 11 o'clock. We found there Marie Beerbohm, Picasso, Madame Picasso, Marie Laurencin, Cocteau, Moise, Radiguet and Brancusi. They were drinking champagne and we joined them . . . the evening was an enormous success and I left for Montparnasse with Brancusi and Radiguet, who had on a dinner jacket. Brancusi lived near Montparnasse and said that he would see me home. We arrived at the Dôme at 5 minutes to 2, just in time to buy some cigarettes. Brancusi had an inspiration. He said to Radiguet and me: 'Let us go to Marseilles now.' I being very stupid said that I must go home. I did not really think that he meant it and went home . . . Brancusi and Radiguet, the latter still in a dinner jacket, took the train for Marseille a few hours later without baggage, just as they were. On the way to Marseille they decided that, being once started, they might as well go on to Corsica. When they arrived at Marseille, Radiguet bought some clothes from a sailors' shop and they took the boat for Corsica. They remained there for 2 weeks.[36]

On their return to Paris Brancusi encountered a certain degree of hostility from some of his friends one evening at the Rotonde. The angriest of course was Radiguet's then lover, Jean Cocteau, who eventually extricated himself from the awkward situation by writing to Brancusi not only that he bore him no grudges but that in fact he approved of such 'types of things'.[37] In a letter dated 22 January 1922, Cocteau apologized to Brancusi for the 'gloomy reception of yesterday' . . . I totally approve of this type of thing and my disgust is only against the slimy arses [*les culs-baveux*] who do not understand anything that is fresh or impulsive.' Cocteau added that he found Radiguet looking superb. Corsica did more for him than the environment of La Rotonde.[38]

Brancusi was very fond of women too. His most famous lover was without doubt Margit Pogany (1870–1964). She met Brancusi in 1910 on arrival in Paris from Budapest to study painting. In spite of Paleolog's mysogynistic remarks she achieved a degree of success in the competitive capital. Thus at the 1910 Salon held at the Grand Palais she was 'in good company alongside Matisse, Duchamp, Duchamp-Villon and Lehmbruck with two paintings: *Nature morte* and *Femme lisant*'.[39] Her relationship with Brancusi spanned 26 years (1911–37), and *La Dation Brancusi 2001* contains nineteen letters and one postcard from her.[40] They testify to an affectionate relationship that matured from youthful romance to lasting friendship. On one occasion Brancusi openly confessed his love to Paleolog, who in 1915 was travelling on a diplomatic passport to Budapest, where Pogany was living at that time: 'And you tell her, what I told you, that I loved her and I love her – after Ioana I did not love anybody else'.[41]

An unusual relationship developed between Brancusi and Eileen Lane, who arrived in Paris from America in 1922 and was introduced to Brancusi by Lizica Codreanu. Eileen had just broken off an engagement, and in order to cheer her up Brancusi invited her to accompany him on a trip to Romania (11 September to 7 October). This was in a way Brancusi's second escapade that year, following his 'elopement' to Corsica with Radiguet in January. A rather curious detail links the two occasions, namely the fact that in each instance Brancusi pretended to be the father of his much younger companion. Thus when on board ship to Corsica, Brancusi asked the patron of its restaurant: 'Tell me sir, it is not for me that I am asking but for my son, can one find a girl here for him?'[42] A few months later and he was telling Eileen 'Don't worry, I am going to present you as my daughter.' She remembered with great affection the luxurious train voyage that took them to Romania, from whence they visited Tîrgu Jiu and Peştişani, where Brancusi had been at school. On the return journey they stopped in Rome and stayed at the Savoy Hotel, and then in Marseille at the Hotel Splendid.[43]

Brancusi was obviously simply making mischief when on board ship in the restaurant, but the second case seems at first less easy to explain, for it would have been unsettling not only for Eileen but also for Brancusi's family and friends in Peştişani to have Brancusi present her there as his daughter. His family would have been the first to know if Brancusi had married, or even settled down, never mind fathered a child. Once again, his remark must have been in jest, because in a letter to his brother Dumitru written immediately after the visit, Brancusi refers to Eileen Lane in a formal manner as 'Mlle Lane', and in its *post scriptum* adds 'Mlle Lane was enchanted and she is sending you her best wishes and affectionately embraces the nieces'.[44]

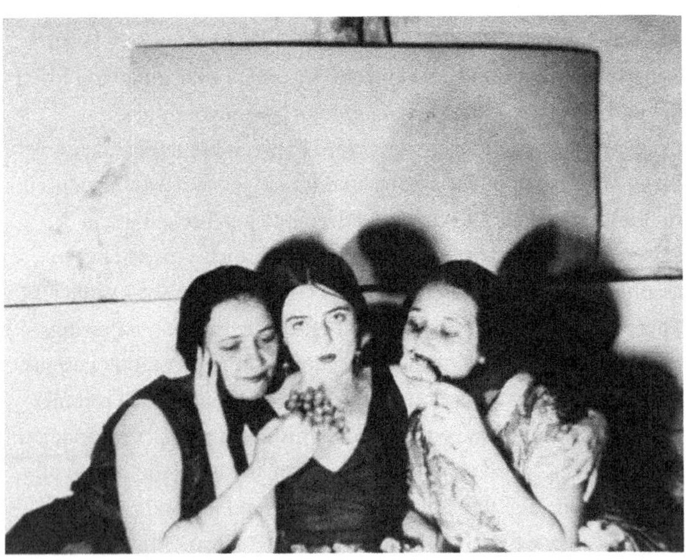

Eileen Lane and the Codreanu sisters in Brancusi's studio in 1922.

Eileen Lane soon returned to America and married a Howard Martindale Kinney. But she reappeared briefly in Paris the following year. In a letter to Brancusi of 30 October 1923, written after the visit, she reveals that it was more than just filial love she felt for him, and that he clearly reciprocated her sentiments: 'I had profound pleasure in seeing you again, but I had also the pain of seeing you suffer. I was saddened by a fear of showing an affection that I no longer have the right to show.'[45]

Other relationships in the 1920s included his affair with Marthe Lebherz, *La blonde Iseult* as he liked to call her. The daughter of an affluent Swiss physician, in order to camouflage their secret liaison from her respectable family Brancusi employed her during his first visit to New York in 1926 as his 'private secretary'. The impressive correspondence between them in the *Dation Brancusi 2001* reveals Brancusi's love for the young woman he affectionately called *Tonton* in their moments of intimacy while Brancusi himself was *Tantan*, which is how Marthe must have referred to him. (Brancusi even intended to write a book entitled *L'Histoire d'amour de Tonton et Tantan* and to that effect kept all Marthe's letters in chronological order locked in a suitcase.) It was as passionate a relationship as it was short; by 1928 it had come to its natural end.[46]

But among Brancusi's numerous lovers, a very special place must be given to the English concert pianist Vera Moore, whom the 54-year-old Brancusi met in 1930. In 1934 their son John was born, although Brancusi was never to acknowledge him. Nevertheless, Brancusi's relationship with Moore continued until his death in 1957. *La Dation Brancusi 2001* has 'forty documents in its possession, revealing that Vera Moore was Brancusi's last and one of his greatest loves'.[47] At a more mundane level Brancusi established close friendships with a number of rich society women, among whom were Léonie Ricou, Mme Eugène Meyer Jr, Baroness Renée Irana Frachon and Nancy Cunard as well as Peggy Guggenheim.[48] He also made portraits of some of his lovers as well as his friends and patrons.

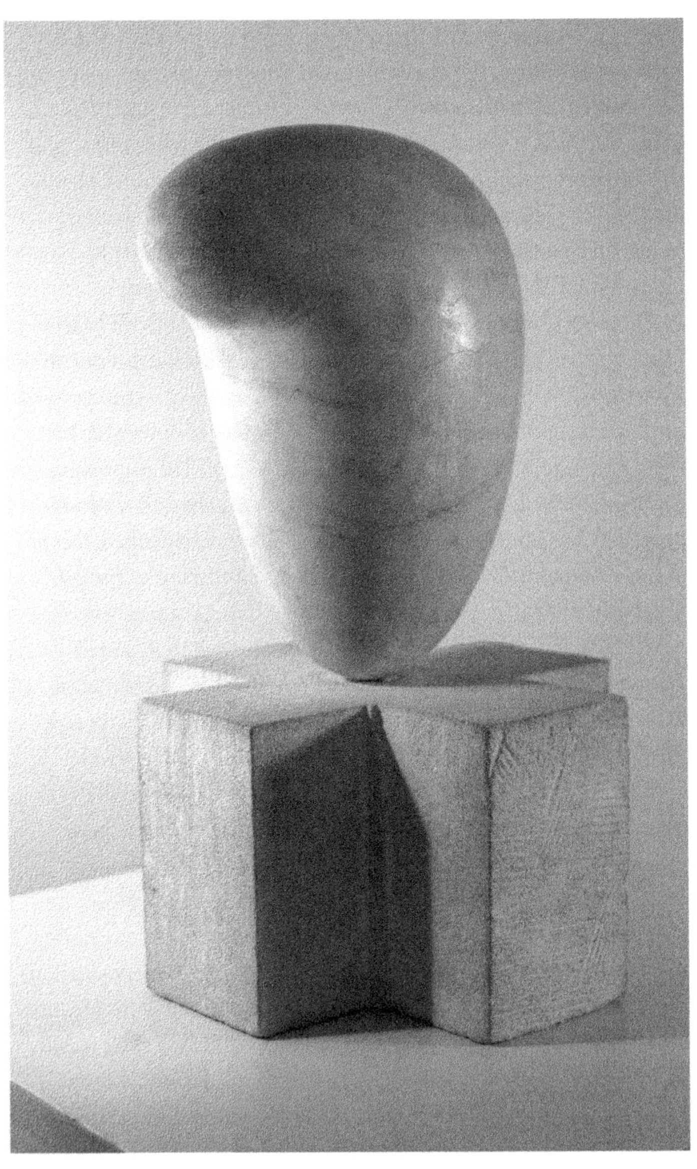

Eileen Lane, 1923.

Among them the most enduring are obviously *Mlle Pogany* and *Princess X.* Nancy Cunard is *Jeune fille sophistique* and Léonie Ricou is *Mme L. R.*

Brancusi's detestation of academic portraiture is well known, but if we return to his earliest portraits, such as the portrait of Victoria Vaschide of 1905 (now known only from photographs),[49] we can trace his path away from naturalistic representation. What we see in the case of Victoria Vaschide is a realistic rendering of a pretty young woman wearing a fashionable hairstyle.[50] From there we can glimpse the period of transition from academic portraiture to his later idiosyncratic portraits via two seminal examples: *Portrait of Renée Franchon* and *Mlle Pogany*. In both instances the final result still bears a *Gestaltic* resemblance to their sitters, but this was no longer to be the case in Brancusi's subsequent portraits of women. So what kind of visual relationship can be established – even with the best will in the world – between the wooden totem topped by a tuft (whose title, *Mme L. R.,* is certainly a statement of intent by Brancusi) and a photograph of the beautiful socialite Léonie Ricou?[51] An explanation may be gleaned from Brancusi himself. Among the handful of aphorisms he left us, one in particular is worth quoting here: 'Simplicity is not an aim in art but we arrive at simplicity in spite of ourselves in approaching the real meaning of things.'[52]

Like his friend Erik Satie, Brancusi discovered Plato's *Dialogues*, and his search for 'essences' reflects Plato's idealist philosophy. This may well have occurred under the influence of Satie's research for *La Mort de Socrate*. Both used a recent translation of Plato's dialogues in French by Victor Cousin, which Satie adapted in his idiosyncratic manner.[53] Indeed, a glance at the inventory of Brancusi's personal library reveals a number of interesting preferences. He bought both literature and poetry, above all those by his friends, to whom he showed his loyalty and respect by collecting the books, essays and magazines they wrote, produced or edited. Among them we find works by Apollinaire, Cendrars, Cocteau, Duchamp, Paul Morand, Man Ray, André Salmon and Tristan Tzara.[54] Brancusi's interest in contemporary philosophy is restricted to writings by Henri Bergson and the mathematician Henri Poincaré. He owned Bergson's two seminal books, both published in 1914, *Matière et memoire* and *L'Evolution créatrice*, in which there are some heavily underlined passages in pencil in chapter Three, 'De la signification de la vie, l'order de la nature et la forme de l'intelligence'. Brancusi was also interested in newly evolved theories of the fourth dimension postulated by Henri Poincaré, whose writings became fashionable among artists, as did the study and understanding of science and technology, reflected in Brancusi and Duchamp's own fascination with issues such as flight and aeroplanes. There are four books by Poincaré listed in Brancusi's library that reflect his interest in these fashionable ideas: *La Valeur de la science*, *Science et méthode*, *La Science et l'hypothèse* and *Dernières pensées*.[55]

Some of the books in the library have been removed since they were inventoried and among them went a volume of Plato's *Dialogues*. But against item 118 of the inventory list we find the following note, 'Oeuvres de Platon (couverture)', which may have been the cover of a collection of dialogues published by Classique Garnier that contained the following dialogues: *Ion, Lysis, Protagoras, Phaedrus* and the *Symposium*.[56]

So are Brancusi's portraits of his female sitters the material embodiment of Platonic essences? 'All my life I have sought the essence of flight', Brancusi confessed to his friend, the biographer Carola Giedion-Welcker,[57] but his quest may well have been for the ultimate Platonic essence, the essence of being. In the *Symposium* Socrates repeats a speech about love that he once heard from a woman from Mantinea, Diotima, as his contribution to the discourses on the theme of love selected as the topic of debate at that particular symposium. In her conclusion Diotima asks an admiring Socrates:

What may we suppose to be the felicity of the man who sees
absolute beauty in its essence, pure and unalloyed, who, instead
of a beauty tainted by human flesh and colour and a mass of
perishable rubbish, is able to apprehend divine beauty where
it exists apart and alone. Do you think that it will be a poor life
that a man leads who has his gaze fixed in that direction, who
contemplates absolute beauty with the appropriate faculty and
is in constant union with it?[58]

Echoes of this belief in the apprehension of absolutes can be found
in one of Brancusi's well-known aphorisms:

I give you pure joy. Look at my sculptures until you see them.
Those closest to God have seen them. Being close to God is to
leave behind the contingent, is to tackle the principle, the essence
of things, is to steer one's eyes towards the absolute.[59]

His words provide the golden key to unlocking the mysterious
physical shapes the portraits maintain and to understanding them
in their essential rather than contingent manifestation.

7

Tîrgu-Jiu

In 1934 the National League of the Romanian Women of Gorj
proposed a monument to honour the soldiers who lost their lives
during World War I when defending the town of Tîrgu-Jiu against
Germany's armies. The commission was offered to the sculptor
Militza Petrascu, who had already completed a public monument
in Tîrgu-Jiu, a classical sarcophagus ornamented with reliefs,
dedicated to a local heroine, Ecaterina Teodoroiu. Petrascu
refused it and suggested that her former *maître*, Brancusi,
should undertake the commission instead.[1] She subsequently
wrote to Brancusi regarding this proposal, and in his reply he
expressed his pleasure at being able to do something for his
native Romania:

Your letter made me very happy. Please excuse my late reply but
I wanted instead of replying to you to surprise you by coming to
Romania myself. I had such nostalgia to see our plains covered in
snow, which I had not seen since my childhood. I wanted at the
same time to try and organize an exhibition in Bucharest, but I
was sick at the last minute and a heap of muddles made my trip
impossible I have decided to arrive in May and I cannot tell you
how happy I am to be able to make something in this country of
ours. I would like to thank you as well as Mme Tataresco for this
privilege. In fact all my works which have started such a long time
ago are now reaching their end and I feel like an apprentice on

the threshold of becoming a master – thus the proposal could not have come at a better moment.[2]

For this project, which required sound craftsmanship backed by technology, Brancusi enlisted the collaboration of Ştefan Georgescu-Gorjan, the son of his childhood friend Ion. While on a visit to Brancusi's studio in January 1935, Brancusi mentioned the Tîrgu-Jiu project to the young engineer. It was 'an ardent desire of his, which was on the point of becoming not too remote a possibility'.[3]

Brancusi arrived in Tîrgu-Jiu in the summer of 1937, and Ştefan Georgescu-Gorjan remembered how on 25 July Brancusi invited him for a walk around the site selected for the *Column without End*. 'I don't remember whether the name of the wasteland bordered with low houses and covered with large haystacks was in common use during our "shop talks" about the Column', Georgescu-Gorjan recalled, 'but in the following months Brancusi and I called the place chosen for the column the "Haymarket".' Subsequently the engineer took a photograph of the deserted field that became the background for the original outline of the *Column without End* drawing in Brancusi's hand.[4]

Although work on the *Column* started in 1937, its conception goes back, as Brancusi confessed to Petrascu in his letter, to 'a long time ago'. Carola Giedion-Welcker recalled that, back in 1916, fascinated by the ways in which trees seeded and flourished, 'in three days Brancusi made his first column from a kind of trunk of an imposing tree'.[5] Although Giedion-Welcker's claim can only be supported by photographs, 1916 is almost certainly the year in which Brancusi executed his first column. It was followed by several additional examples in wood, which in turn led to the stainless-steel and cast-iron masterpiece erected at Tîrgu-Jiu.[6] Among them only one column is well documented: the nine-module wood column Brancusi made to be placed in the garden of his friend, the American photographer Edward Steichen, who lived in Voulangis on the outskirts of Paris.

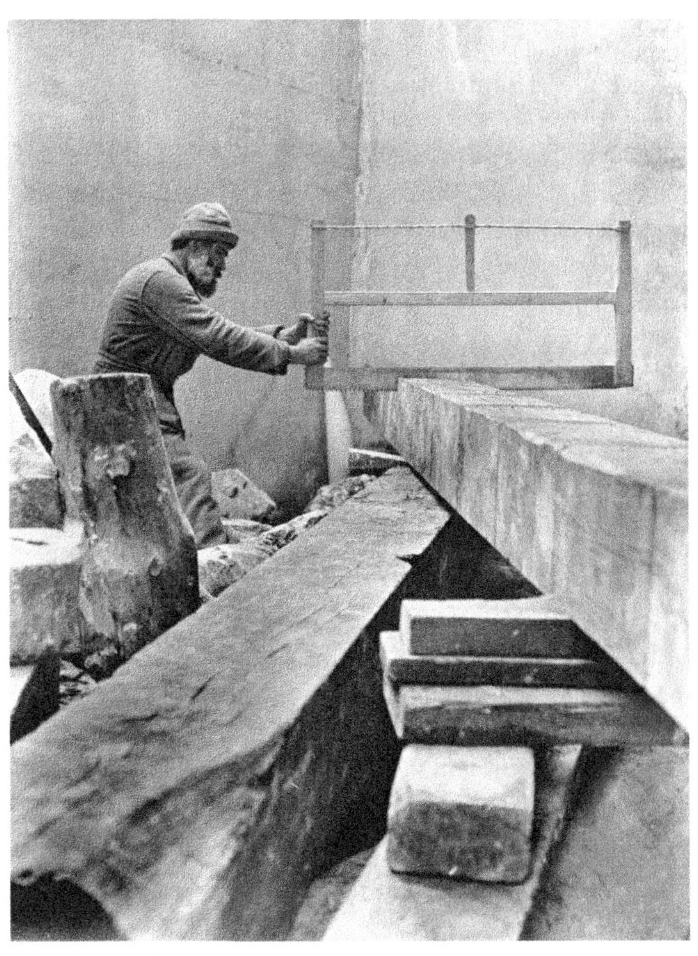

Brancusi working on a *Column without End* in his studio, *c.* 1924. This is the 9-m-high wooden column that was to be placed in the garden of his friend, the photographer Edward Steichen, at Voulangis.

After Steichen had returned to America, Brancusi removed the
column from the deserted villa, first sawing it into two smaller, uneven
halves. Man Ray, who photographed Brancusi in action at Voulangis,
recalled the event:

> Steichen had returned to the States for good, abandoning his
> house in the country. Brancusi wished to recover a sculpture
> that had been left in the garden. It was a wooden trunk about
> thirty feet high, carved with zigzag notches, called 'The Column
> Without End'. I came around to his studio with my car; he got
> in carrying a large coil of rope and a saw. The house looked very
> sad, as do all abandoned houses, with some old empty frames
> lying around and the garden overgrown with weeds. But the
> column stood proudly in the middle like some prehistoric totem
> pole awaiting a ritual.

Very quickly Brancusi cut the column into two halves:

> But the cut was perfectly horizontal and the sculpture held in
> place as if it hadn't been cut. . . . There were about three feet
> more in the ground, he said, but it did not matter – it was the
> Column Without End, whatever its length. Next day he would
> send a truck out to bring the two pieces in. They could always
> be put together again. Someday he'd make one in metal.[7]

And so he did! Structurally the *Column without End* consists of
fifteen modules or *beads*, as Brancusi liked to call them, flanked
at each end by half modules. Its execution is well documented by
Ştefan Georgescu-Gorjan. Initially Brancusi produced a wooden
module that gave him problems: 'Long and numerous were the days
when Brancusi patiently wrung from the wood, fibre by fibre, shaving
by shaving, the excess, the chrysalis cover, hiding the much anticipated surfaces of the rhomboid.'[8] The module was completed at

the end of August, after which Brancusi had to return to Paris, but work on the Column started almost immediately without him.

The *Column without End* consists of a steel metallic core in three separate sections welded together with a square section, with a side of 40 cm rooted in a pyramidal steel base encased in concrete 5 metres below ground level which constitutes the invisible base. Above ground the column consists of 15 'beads' strung out on the stainless steel core just like beads on a string, plus two half 'heads' flanking it at both ends. The ratio established by Brancusi was 1:2:4 (side of the base; central width; height), but it was Georgescu-Gorjan who had to work out the exact mathematical proportions of the individual beads, which he established as 45 x 90 x 180 cm. This determined the maximum potential height of the *Column* – almost 30 metres – that it could be without disintegrating, so that a harmonious whole emerges from carefully calculated proportions. As the engineer explained:

> The formula 1:2:4 give the plastic harmony of the element. The formula ½ + 15 + ½ is the arithmetical expression of the number of whole elements and of the two semi-elements, which give the column its appropriate height, its slenderness and élan. The secret of the *Column without End* is hidden in these two formulae.[9]

Brancusi specifically expressed in a letter of 20 September 1935 sent from Paris to Georgescu-Gorjan what the colour of the *Column* should be 'The metalization must be yellow. Have you cast the elements?'[10] But while the Column might without difficulty be understood to represent a prominent cenotaph to the fallen, albeit uncompromising in its unprecedented form, the other commemorative components that form part of the Tîrgu-Jiu complex – the *Gate of the Kiss*, the *Table of Silence*, and the stools and benches that flank the alley leading from the *Gate* to the bank of the River Jiu – are gnomic. It appears that whereas from the outset Brancusi's intention was to erect a

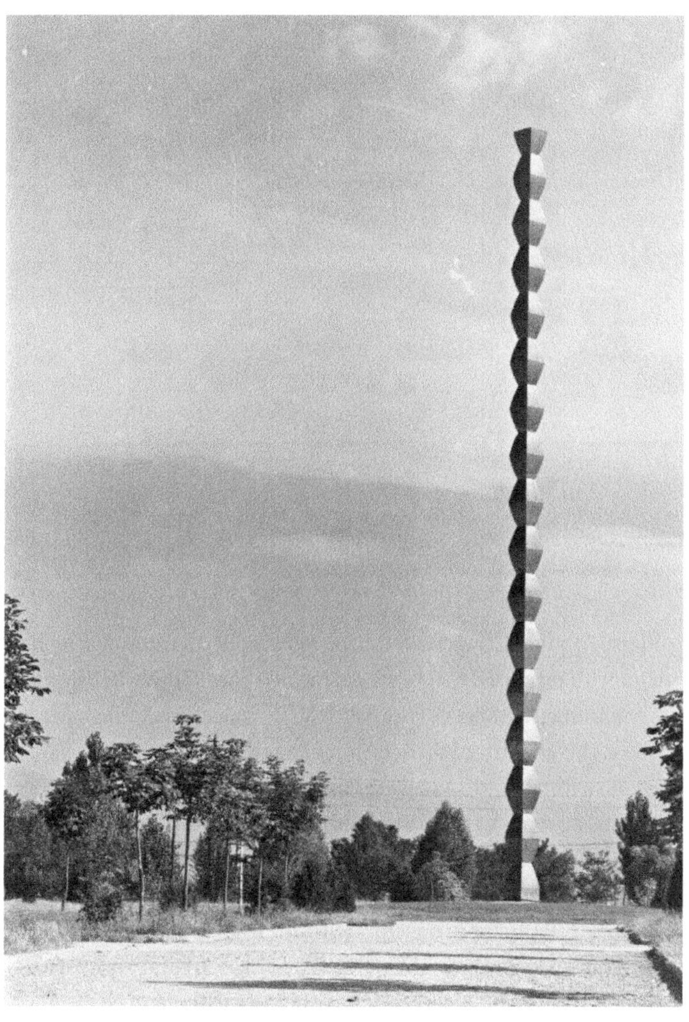

The *Column without End* was regarded by Brancusi as the crowning achievement of his career. Commissioned by Arethie Tătărăscu, wife of the then prime minister, it commemorated the Romanians who died in battle during the First World War. Brancusi initially carved a wooden module and engineer Ştefan Georgescu-Gorjan executed the monument.

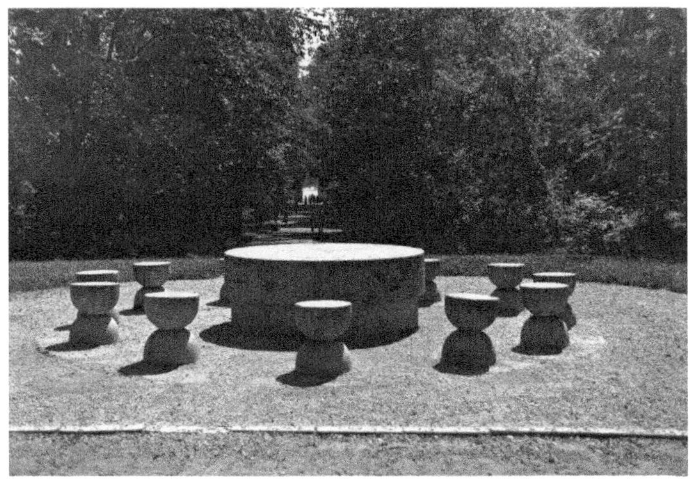

The Table of Silence, 1937–8 and (opposite) *The Gate of the Kiss*, 1937. The three works (*Column, Table, Kiss*), placed on an axis that links the River Jiu with the Hay Market, are now known as the Tîrgu-Jiu Complex.

column, Arethie Tătărăscu had always envisioned a triumphal arch. So Brancusi promised that he would include one.[11] Thus when he met the committee members of the National League of the Romanian Women of Gorj, he told them he intended to erect not just the 'Column without End' but also 'a Portal'. (They, apparently, even suggested he replace the *Column* with a Cockerel, but he refused, explaining that '*Le Coq galique* is not the Romanian cock. The cock does not wear the military mantle in Romanian symbolism. I prefer an infinite column for commemorating the dead.'[12])

Initially the stone portal intended to placate Arethie Tătărăscu was to be placed at the park entrance, but twice Brancusi changed his mind: first he relocated it to a site about 15 metres inside the park, and the foundations were made, but he then decided on another spot, the current ground on which the portal stands.[13]

Work on the 'triumphal arch'–'portal'–'kissing gate', as it was variously called, started in October 1937 while Brancusi was in

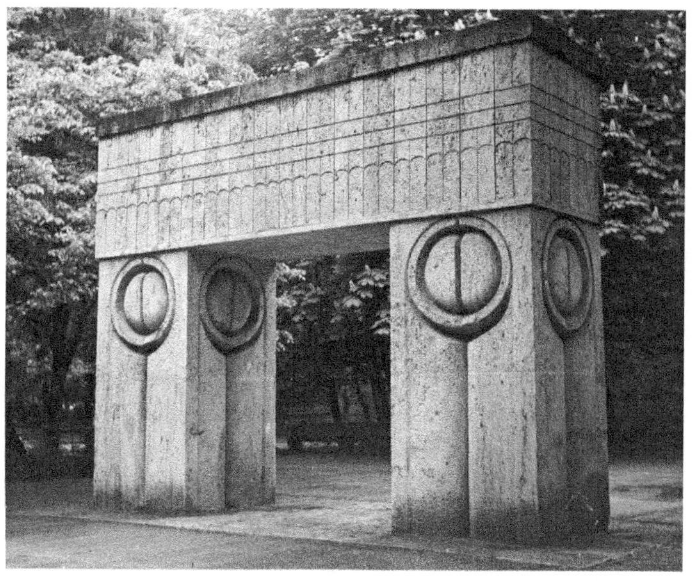

Tîrgu-Jiu. On the sixteenth of that month a notice appeared in
Gorjanul, the local newspaper, announcing that Mme Arethie
Tătărăscu 'wishes to inform the public of her decision to offer the
town a column and a stone portal, the works of the great sculptor
from Gorj, Brancusi'. In November the town council approved the
project: 'an alley starting from the river Jiu, and passing through
a portal to mark the entrance into the public garden', finishing in
'a monument of gratitude consisting of a column of approximately
29 metres height'.[14] Brancusi returned to Paris that same month,
at which point a circular Banpotoc table was already in position by
the river-bank, but no mention of the third component appears in
documents of that year. After trips to India (in pursuit of a temple
commission that collapsed when the interested maharajah suddenly
died), Olanda and America in the first half of 1938, Brancusi returned
to Tîrgu-Jiu in June to attend the spray-metalizing of the *Column
without End* and to complete the *Gate of the Kiss* as well as the round

table and stools. Thirty-two stools in the form of a clepsydra, made
of the same local Banpotoc travertine as the *Gate of the Kiss* were
ordered: thirty square stools to be placed in the niches flanking the
alley (three in each of the ten niches) and twelve round stools to be
placed around the table, which consisted of two superimposed slabs
of stone.[15] The expanse Brancusi required for the complex was later
explained by V. G. Paleolog:

> The statues of Brancusi required large spaces to be adequately
> presented. Their natural monumentality demands a space
> responsive to the rhythm of their proportions, which is always
> *a largo, a maiestoso*. Brancusi experimented with ways of creating
> space required by his works but with the architectural elements
> of sculpture, especially with the purest of his statues. Such is the
> Tîrgu-Jiu ensemble . . . where he built a replica of the *Column
> without End* . . . as well as a *Gate of the Heroes* which opens
> towards the location of the *Round Table*.[16]

Brancusi's friend and fellow Romanian Ionel Jianou immediately
recognized that the *Table of Silence*'s twelve stools were 'reminiscent
of peasant furniture'.[17]

In the summer of 1938 a young stonemason from Bucharest, Ion
Alexandrescu, arrived at Tîrgu-Jiu to assist Brancusi in carving the
frieze of the *Gate* on the lintel of the portal. His account of the experience shows the rigour with which Brancusi approached his work:

> As we decided, I would come to Brancusi's hotel every morning
> at 9 a.m. He had a room on the ground floor, very simply
> furnished: a bed, a wash-basin, a simple cupboard, two kitchen
> chairs, a small table, a suitcase near the cupboard – and a lot
> of empty space on the parquet floor. He would unfold a large
> sheet of paper about two square metres on the carpet and draw
> on it with charcoal fastened on a long walking-stick whilst seated

on the kitchen chair, or standing. He would draw on paper
a series of simple or intertwined lines, formed of leaves, apple
leaves, shaded in the middle as if it were an entry into something
illuminated; on another paper he would draw a kind of long flame
made up of almost straight lines. Then I could not understand a
thing of what he was sketching but I did not have the courage to
ask anything.[18]

They worked for three to four hours every day, after which Brancusi
liked to go to the local market. He always carried cameras and would
both photograph and film the peasants as they chattered, haggled
and hurried about. He also enjoyed photographing everyday domestic
utensils, such as plates, jugs, pots and wooden spoons, as well as
costumes, especially women's folk costumes. Sometimes he and
Alexandrescu walked in the fields, when 'he would photograph
the ears of corn or the allotments with all sorts of flowers'. On their
wanderings Brancusi paused 'whenever he saw peasants eating in the
shade of their carts and would talk to them', and he 'photographed
or filmed them as they worked'[19]

Alexandrescu also recalled Brancusi explaining the rather cryptic
iconographical analysis the master supplied to him of the Tîrgu-Jiu
trilogy (an explication that was too esoteric for Alexandrescu to
comprehend, as he admitted):

Man's path in life starts from the family, from the parental
home. You take several paths, passing from stage to stage, some
bewitched by love, some in pursuit of endless glory. This is the
table and stools, namely the family which disappears and is left
in silence but unforgettable. The crossed paths, the separated
roads, the grouped stools . . . the Gate of the Kiss is the last stage
of youth. By this one can understand many things. Man loves
life, himself; the benches are a long road, the road of life towards
endless glory – symbolized by the Column.[20]

The overall plan of the ensemble is conceived as a straight axis crossing the town and linking the *Column* in the centre of the Hay Market through to the *Gate* situated inside the public gardens, from which an alley flanked by the 30 square clepsidra stools placed in groups of three in niches on each side lead finally to the *Table of Silence* placed by the river-bank. A majestic overall concept perhaps, but at the time when the various parts were being placed in position it was rendered problematic by the Church of the Holy Apostles situated in the middle of the axis that linked the *Column* to the *Gate* to the *Table*. Brancusi appealed to Mme Tătărăscu and the League of the Romanian Women about this and other compromising intrusions and was assured that the church would be removed to another location and that his additional concerns would be dealt with. But in October 1938 when Brancusi returned to Tîrgu-Jiu for the inauguration of the completed complex, he discovered that the promises had not been kept: the church remained in place, the proposed deviation of the railway track, which passed behind the *Column*, had not been carried out, and the trees meant to blank the Avenue of the Heroes had not been planted.[21] To add insult to injury, Mme Tătărăscu had invited King Carol II of Romania to attend the ceremony of the blessing of the church, almost certainly in a diplomatic attempt to deflect attention from the anticipated negative impact of Brancusi's modernist work. King Carol duly arrived, and duly avoided the complex, attending only the religious ceremony.

In its final version the tripartite sculptural grouping comprised the *Column*, *Gate* and *Table*, but it turned out that the conservative intelligentsia of Tîrgu-Jiu was far from ready for such uncompromising modernism. Ionel Jianou noted that the crowd that gathered for the inauguration included numerous persons, who were utterly nonplussed. They 'shrieked with laughter' before a monument that to them was incomprehensible, although 'the peasants liked it well enough because they recognized the ancestral forms of their own folk architecture'. The conservative supporters of academic art were, perhaps not surprisingly, dismayed, while, true to form, Romania's fascist press, following the lead given by Nazi Germany, began campaigning against degenerate art, pointing to Tîrgu-Jiu's new monuments as a perfect collective example of it. The sculptor was 'thoroughly disgusted, but his only response to his opponents' denigrations was a scornful smile'.[22]

Despite this clamour of opposition, Brancusi remained proud of his collaboration with Georgescu-Gorjan. He had in fact dreamed of an even higher column, 'a gigantic' one, long before Tîrgu-Jiu. Back in 1926, during a visit to New York to attend the opening of his exhibition at the Brummer Gallery, Brancusi had been interviewed by Flora Merrill for *The New York World*, and he spoke then of his ambition to build a 'Column of Infinity' in Central Park. 'It would be greater than any building, three times higher than your obelisk in Washington, with a base correspondingly wide – sixty metres or more.' It would be made of metal, and 'in each pyramid there would be apartments and people would live there, and on the very top, I would have my bird – a great bird poised on the top of my infinite Column'.[23] There is a clear parallel here between this megalomaniacal idea and one by that magnificent visionary dreamer the Russian Constructivist Vladimir Tatlin (1885–1953). Tatlin's proposed Monument to the Third International had been commissioned in 1919 by the Department of Fine Arts to be erected in the centre of Moscow, and indeed one of the three models made was shown at the Exhibition of the Eighth Congress of the Soviets in December of the following year. The proposed glass and metal monument, which was to be twice the height of the Empire State Building, was envisaged as a spiral framework supporting a tripartite body (cylinder, cone, cube) suspended on a mobile asymmetrical axis. The cylinder, which was to revolve on its axis once a year, would be a lecture and conference theatre; the cone, moving once a month, would house executive meetings; while the cube, which was to revolve once a day, would serve as an information centre.[24] Not surprisingly, Tatlin's idea was reckoned utterly impracticable: the project was scrapped. It is then startling to learn that, for a time, Brancusi's project had some potential, courtesy of an admirer, a Chicago lawyer named Barnet Hodes, who in 1955 indicated his willingness to finance a column of up to 122 metres to be built on Chicago's Lake Michigan shore. But Brancusi, who by this time was in poor health, explained in a letter of 5 November 1956 that he now envisaged nothing less than a column of 400 metres of stainless steel, 'which will be one of the wonders of the world'.[25] Not unexpectedly, as with Tatlin's Monument to the Third International, Brancusi's Chicago column was never to see the light of day.

Brancusi had returned to Paris from Tîrgu-Jiu rebuffed, and a depressed silence is said by Brancusi's friend and biographer Ionel Jianou to have ensued and endured. In an essay written in 1982, Jianou insisted that the silence he refers to continued even beyond Brancusi's lifetime. According to Jianou, after 1938 Brancusi never again mentioned the complex. Not a word to Malvina Hoffman, who wrote about him in her book *Sculpture Inside and Out* published in 1939; nothing to David Lewis, who published his book on Brancusi in 1957 after several interviews with the sculptor. He was silent on the matter when with Christian Zervos, responsible for *Cahiers d'Art* a *Homage à Brancusi*, and in the company of Carola Giedion-Welcker, who visited Brancusi often during the last years of his life and published her monograph on him in 1959. In support of his claim concerning the silence of Tîrgu-Jiu, Jianou pointed out that

in Zervos's book *The Table of Silence* is neither reproduced nor mentioned. In David Lewis's book we see it in a photograph given him by Brancusi with the following caption: 'Table, seats, gate, 1937, Targu-Jiu, Romania'. In the monograph by Carola Giedion-Welcker the same photograph is reproduced with the caption: 'Table de Pierre et sieges, parc avec *la Porte du Baiser*, 1937, Targu-Jiu Carpathes'.[26]

The long silence that Jianou says lasted no less than 'twenty-five years' can of course only refer to the span between 1938 when Brancusi left Tîrgu-Jiu and the publication in 1963 of Jianou's first monograph on Brancusi, published six years after the sculptor's death. It is interesting, then, to notice that in this first edition of his monograph, Jianou uses two quotations from Malvina Hoffman's book of 1939, in which she records Brancusi earlier telling her proudly about his ongoing work at Tîrgu-Jiu:

> Nature creates plants that grow up straight and strong from the ground: here is my Column . . . Its forms are the same from the ground to the top. It has no need of pedestal or base to support it. The wind will not destroy it; it stands by its own strength . . . In a few days I hope to see this installed in Romania: it is thirty m. high and you know that my friend there once told me that he had never been aware of the great beauty of his garden until he had placed my Column there. It had opened his eyes . . . that is what artists are here for . . . to reveal beauty.[27]

Brancusi also mentioned the Gate of the Kiss to Hoffman, and specifically the engraved frieze on the lintel and the egg motif on the pillars: 'First came the group of two interlaced seated figures in stone . . . then the symbol of the egg, then the thought grew into this gateway to a beyond.'[28] Brancusi's moments of voluble pride concerning his designs for Tîrgu-Jiu seem soon after to have been compromised by the cruel reception of his Romanian master-piece. Yet we find Brancusi's friend of many years, the expatriate Irish writer James Joyce, referring to it in *Finnegans Wake* (1939) as 'hierarchitectitiptitoploftical' and 'celescalating the himals', which might be translated as 'hierarchic architecture with the superior extremity like a proud pinnacle climbing into the sky of very high mountains'.[29]

In the spring of 1939 Brancusi made a trip to America, which lasted approximately a month, after which he returned to Paris. Europe's skies were by then darkening, and the Second World War broke out in September, when Germany invaded Poland, forcing France and Great Britain and their empires to declare war on Germany. On 14 June 1940 Germany's armies stormed into Paris and within days France had collapsed. By then Brancusi was in his sixties. He remained at his white ateliers in Montparnasse. He lived quietly, surrounded by his sculptures. Work continued, albeit at a slow pace: two bronze versions of *The Bird in Space*, a stone version of *The Kiss*, a new version of *The Miracle* in veined grey marble, and one new work in white marble, *The Flying Turtle*, which followed on from a wood version of two years previously. (In 1955, when the marble version of *The Flying Turtle* was sent to the Guggenheim Museum in New York to be exhibited at their Brancusi retrospective, it was mistakenly displayed upside down, much to Brancusi's mortification.[30]) The war years were a time when Brancusi returned to *animalier* sculpture.

8

Last Works, Last Friends, Legacy

Five years after the war ended in 1945, but at a time when life in Paris remained somewhat austere, the English architect and writer David Lewis visited Brancusi: 'The experience of visiting his studio was that of visiting an island where calm and equilibrium reigned.' This was Brancusi's oasis, a personal refuge that had protected him from the war and its atrocities. In his seventies now, Brancusi appeared to the young Englishman like a serene ancient, 'a short, sinewy, patriarchal figure in a jacket, trousers and soft sun hat of calico. He would be smoking a thin cigar in a charred holder. His grey-white beard was stained round the edges with nicotine. His small eyes were alternatively direct, restless, observant, then deeply ruminative.'[1] When Lewis quizzed Brancusi 'about the German occupation of Paris', Brancusi replied: "The war! The war marched up and down rue Vaugirard!" Not up or down impasse Ronsin, he seems to have been saying.

> One is aware of repair garages, and the strident air-assaulting noise of panel-beating! The contrast with Brancusi's street is absolute. The impasse Ronsin, a little cul-de-sac, is a country lane. At the further end are trees and a gate.

Brancusi was in fact gradually becoming a recluse, as he himself confessed to Carola Giedion-Welcker in 1946: 'I am no longer of this world, I am far out of myself, detached from my person. I live among

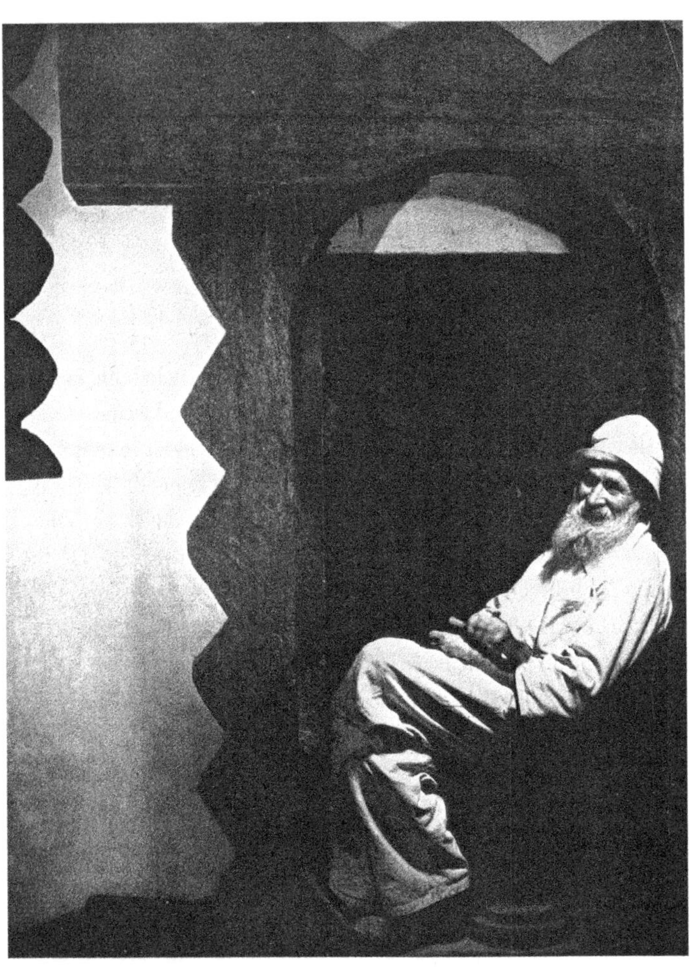

Brancusi by his *Porte Sculptée*, 1955.

the essential things.'[2] According to the American poet William Carlos Williams:

> The man, now well over 70, living alone, as he has always lived, in his studio, has now become famous for his broiled steaks cooked by himself at his own fire, which he himself serves as though he were a shepherd at night on one of his native hillsides under the stars. A white collie named Polaire used to be his constant companion reinforcing the impression of a shepherd which, with his shaggy head of hair, broad shoulders and habitual reserve, he seemed to his friends to be.[3]

How did others of the avant-garde fare in old age? Picasso, for example, loved women too, but unlike Brancusi he created some of the most frankly erotic, even pornographic (some would argue) images of his entire career very late in life. Georges Braque, who died in 1963, had for years locked himself in his studio, which became the main subject-matter of his paintings, and created a sombre microcosm conducive to ruminations about the transitoriness of life; a sort of *memento mori* minus the human skull and snuffed candle. Like others of that generation of artists who were instrumental in shaping the European avant-garde – Matisse, Léger, Miró – Brancusi continued to work creatively during the difficult period when Europe was at war, albeit at a slower pace, preferring to revisit old motifs. In the aftermath of the war, however, Paris was beginning to present a different picture altogether. Two seminal factors that could be singled out as the main contributors to this state of affairs are the following: the shift in the balance of power dominating the art world from Paris to New York; and the Cold War. In the former case economic pressures dictated. By 1948 Clement Greenberg, the self-styled official voice of the newly emerging American avant-garde, declared in the January issue of the influential left-wing magazine *The Partisan Review* that 'One has the impression – but only the impression

– that the immediate future of Western art, if it is to have an immediate future, depends on what is done in this country.' Backing Greenberg's observation was the emergence of the first all-American avant-garde movement, Abstract Expressionism, which, Greenberg argued, showed 'a capacity for fresh content that does not seem to be matched either in France or Great Britain'.[4]

Meanwhile artists in Paris were faced with a new task in the awareness that they needed to find a new language that reflected post-war conditions. They needed to formulate a fresh foundation for art in response to the pressing new social and ethical issues that had come to the fore in the 1930s and early '40s.[5] As a consequence, at the end of the 1940s some artists, such as André Fougeron, were still advocating a militant realist art, but there was also the re-emergence of abstraction. And in 1948 André Breton, Jean Paulhan, Charles Rattan, Henri-Pierre Roché and Michel Tapié together with Jean Dubuffet founded the Compagnie d'Art Brut, which promoted works produced by individuals on society's margins, often maladjusted persons, today identified as Outsider art.[6]

The Cold War exacerbated the division between America and Europe by adding a political dimension. Two important articles published in *Artforum* in 1973 and 1974 written by Max Kozloff and Eva Cockroft respectively provide an analysis of the link between Cold War politics and the arts, and the two institutions primarily responsible for promoting American art as a propaganda weapon of the Cold War were the Museum of Modern Art in New York and the CIA. MoMA was founded in 1929 through the backing of Mrs John D. Rockefeller, Jr; its first president was Nelson Rockefeller, and the Rockefeller ideology became adopted by the museum whose political activities during World War Two are well documented. The CIA became involved in cultural activities during the Cold War through Thomas W. Braden, who, having worked for MoMA in 1948–9 as executive secretary joined the CIA in 1950, where he was in charge of its cultural activities for 1951–4. In 1967 he published an article in the *Saturday Evening Post* (20 May) tellingly entitled 'I'm glad the CIA is immoral'. The official line that provided this *rationale* can be summed up by the dichotomy Abstract Expressionism (the USA and its West Europe dependants) versus Socialist Realism (the USSR and its East European satellites).[7]

The debate between realism, represented on the post-war Paris art scene by André Fougeron and the *misérabilisme* of Bernard Buffet and Marcel Gromaire, and abstraction was still in its infancy in 1948–9 in Paris, but within a mere decade it had escalated to heroic proportions. As a consequence the focus of critical debate well charted in the press shifts accordingly from the hitherto dominant theme of figuration versus abstraction to abstraction versus abstraction, whereby the merits or demerits of the impressive array of discourses and theories of abstraction were placed centre stage in the intellectual life of Paris's artistic community. So radical was this shift that in 1957, one year before his death at the age of 81, Brancusi's contemporary Maurice de Vlaminck (1876–1958) wrote an open letter deploring the demise of figurative art. He remained, however, a solitary figure in the wilderness of post-war artistic discourse.[8]

After the war Brancusi's response to the brave new world that was now emerging was to withdraw from it altogether, allowing very few visitors to the studios. Among those who were invited was Sonia Delaunay, who had first met Brancusi in the 1930s. She became a regular visitor. Moreover, she was instrumental in facilitating Brancusi's wish to bequeath his home-cum-workplace to the French government by introducing him to Jean Cassou, at that time chief curator of the Musée d'Art Moderne de la Ville de Paris, who suggested to Brancusi, who was then still a Romanian citizen, that he acquire French citizenship, which he did.[9]

The two other visitors, both women, who were allowed in the inner sanctum were the writer and journalist Dora Vallier and the designer and Surrealist painter Valentine Hugo, both of whom have left accounts. Dora Vallier was aware of her privileged status as a visitor to 'the atelier of this grand sculptor where she knew almost nobody was allowed to visit for some years'. She dated her visit with precision: Friday 4 May 1956. One of her first impressions was of a strange pervasive smell:

> The bitter-sweet smell of the homes of peasants, which I recognized. I forgot Paris and the famous sculptor I came to see. I found myself in a very remote countryside, in the home of a man who lived close to the earth. He has made all the objects which surrounded us with his own hands: his bed: an assembly of boards in white wood; the tabourets, cut from barely reduced trunks of trees, the low circular table, the shelf on which there was a radio, but a disconnected radio, the carcass of lamps and the wires below . . .

And in this home was 'this old man with a white beard who had adopted a prophetic air about him'.

> I have never seen a man living in such an overwhelming solitude, with such a detachment from life, at such a distance from me. In this atmosphere which belonged to him, I was anachronistic, like the telephone which I discovered in a corner.[10]

Valentine Hugo (1897–1968) also left a touching testimony, but unlike other visitors she was brave enough to share her own weaknesses with Brancusi by describing in two letters her own ailing health, loneliness and financial problems. On her first visit to impasse Ronsin, after she passed some 'garages' she reached 'the remains of an abandoned garden', where 'I found the door I was looking for in a charming country lane, filled with leaves and birds':

> What seemed so incredible was that I was barely 50 metres from the inferno and the noise of the city. The door opened after a

short wait and I had the impression, after being announced by the harmonious and grave sound of an invisible bell, that I was entering the atelier calmly although my heart was beating very hard. Suddenly I found myself dazzled by light in an immense white space all vibrating with unknown beings. A man was standing in front of me, it was Brancusi all covered in white from work and sunny from the reflection of the large handwoven cloth, a beard of the same colour was framing his regular features. His eyes were smiling more than his mouth and I whispered under my breath: 'I am Valentine Hugo, I was the friend of Satie and Radiguet and I came to see you and talk about them, I came to see your work after a long time that I dared not but now I am here.'

Her first impression of the sculptures is rendered in an equally poetic language: 'Everything appeared alive around me, everything I had previously seen frozen on paper was now quivering and singing silently.' She noted each white *Cock* 'soaring like a wreath of cries bristling with sparkles', the *Columns without End* 'climbing sombrely in space', each *Bird* was 'spinning' in its flight with 'an élan of infinite grace'. The *Sorceress* and *Caryatid* were there, and the *Grand Fish* in grey marble. 'I was conquered by the *King of Kings*, superb, placed near the beautiful portal which was guarding the passage into the next atelier, where I soon found out was where Brancusi was eating and resting,' As their friendship developed Hugo felt sufficiently at ease to write intimate letters, the first dated 4 March 1956, concerning both her declining health and his and her feelings. In her second letter (Wednesday 7 March) she writes:

Dear friend, dear Brancusi, I want to say to you as my dear Satie once wrote to me: 'you are too good, much too good for me'. . . . When your messenger with incense arrived I had with me two very old friends both of whom visited your atelier some years ago and who are sad that you are suffering so much.

She concludes by promising a visit the following week, addressing him as 'mon incomparable ami, pour me raconter de belles histories et me donner la joie des plus purs de ma vie.'[11]

Brancusi's increasingly frail health was not a new theme. An article entitled 'A Humble Life of Pure Joy' had appeared in *The New York Times* back in 1953 (23 October), giving a touching description of the elderly sculptor. Described as 'wearing white pyjamas and a yellow, gnomelike cap', Brancusi today 'hobbles about his studio tenderly caring for and communing with the silent host of fish, birds, heads and endless columns which he created.' And rather predictably and patronisingly, readers learned, if they didn't know already, that 'the old man leads the same humble life he led as a peasant boy in Romania before the turn of the century.'[12]

Brancusi died on 16 March 1957. At his funeral, which took place at Montparnasse cemetery, where almost half a century earlier Brancusi's *The Kiss* had been placed as a funerary monument, Georges A. Salles, director of the National Museums of France, delivered the graveside speech, one of poignant homage:

> Since we will never again hear that lilting voice which floated up from your beard to transport us to a land of legend, since we will never again see your bright beady eyes which sparkled with mischief and seemed to be laughing at something which they could see and we could not, since we will never again be received in that studio of yours, by a Homeric shepherd in the mist of his fabulous herd, I say therefore farewell . . . I say farewell but your works will remain pure and luminous, they are more alive today than ever, and they will never die.[13]

The works and studio complex that Brancusi bequeathed to France was to present the director of the Musée National d'Art Moderne, Jean Cassou, with an almost bewildering challenge, and over the following years and decades the (eventually dismantled) studios

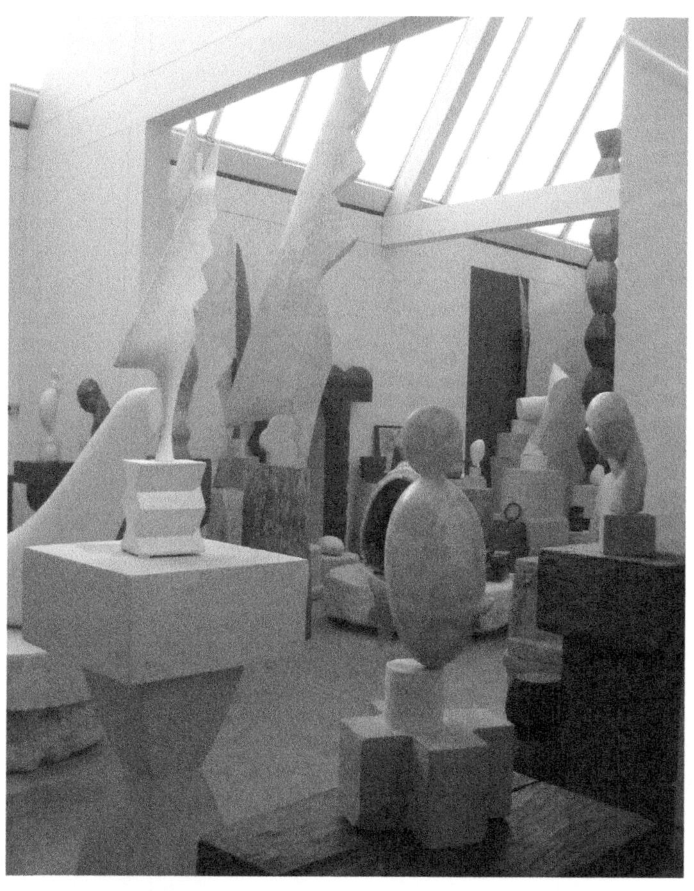

Inside Atelier Brancusi today.

and their works underwent a number of unsuccessful metamorphoses
qua public display that consequently rendered them inaccessible
to visitors for long periods of time. The complex was reopened in
its current form at the Pompidou Centre in 1997 after an ambitious
restoration directed by architect Renzo Piano. To celebrate this event,
a massive and much overdue *catalogue raisonné* of the contents, *La
Collection de l'atelier Brancusi*, was published soon after.[14]

References

Introduction

1 Peter Neagoe, *The Saint of Montparnasse (A Novel Based on the Life of Constantin Brancusi)* (New York, 1965).
2 In the 2003 catalogue by Marielle Tabart and Doina Lemny, *La Dation Brancusi (dessins et archives)*, published for the exhibition held that year at the CNAC, Centre Georges Pompidou, Paris. In 1956 Brancusi bequeathed his five studios in impasse Ronsin with their entire contents to the French Government on condition that they be preserved and incorporated to become part of the National Museum of Modern Art and opened to the public as 'Atelier Brancusi'. See the end of chapter Eight for further details.
3 Eugène Ionesco, 'Par Eugène Ionesco', *Cahiers du musée de poche* (December 1959).
4 Doina Lemny, 'Les Américans à Paris', *La Dation Brancusi*, p. 195.
5 Jeanne Robert Foster, 'Constantin Brancusi: A Note on the Man and the Formal Perfection of his Carvings', *Vanity Fair* (May 1922), pp. 6–8.
6 In *Constantin Brancusi* (Iassy, 2005), Doina Lemny lists three books V. G. Paleolog published during Brancusi's lifetime: *A doua carte despre C. Brancusi* (Craiova, 1944), *Brancusi: Introducere la cunostiinta operei lui C. Brancusi* (Craiova, 1944), and *Constantin Brancusi* (Bucharest, 1947).
7 In 1978 when I met the late V. G. Paleolog in Craiova, he allowed me to take notes from the manuscript of volume II (never published) of his book on the sculptor (volume I of *Brancusi–Brancusi* was published at Craiova in 1976). In chapter One of the MS, entitled 'The Event of my First Meeting with Brancusi', Paleolog describes his initial visit to the studio in 1910 (MS, pp. 3–46).

8 V. G. Paleolog, *Constantin Brancusi* (Bucharest, 1947).

9 Marie Bengesco, 'L'Art en Roumanie', in *La Roumanie en images* (Paris, 1919), p. 33.

10 David Lewis, *Constantin Brancusi* (London, 1957).

11 Christian Zervos, *Constantin Brancusi (sculptures, peintures, fresques, dessins)* (Paris, 1957).

12 Herbert Read, 'Constantin Brancusi, 1876–1957', *The Listener* (4 April 1957), p. 555.

13 Carola Giedion-Welcker, *Constantin Brancusi* (Neuchâtel, 1959).

14 Ionel Jianou, *Constantin Brancusi* (Paris, 1963) and English edn (London, 1963).

15 Jianou, *Constantin Brancusi*, p. 73.

16 For this see Doina Lemny, 'Le Jeu de l'écrit', *La Dation Brancusi*, p. 87.

17 Alexandre Istrati and Natalia Dumitresco, *Brancusi* (Paris, 1986), p. 121.

1 Childhood

1 Ion Mocioi, 'Fiul unui taran roman', in *Constantin Brancusi – Viata* (Jassy, 2003), pp. 7–25.

2 S. Mehedinti, 'Schita geografica', in *Calauza oficiala si catalogul expozitiunei* (Bucharest, 1906), p. 19.

3 George Opresco, *Peasant Art in Romania* (London, 1929), p. 12.

4 Opresco, *Peasant Art in Romania*, p. 15.

5 Opresco, *Peasant Art in Romania*, p. 19.

6 Quoted in Nicolae Iorga, *Istoria Romanilor prin calatori* (Bucharest, 1981), p. 670.

7 Opresco, *Peasant Art in Romania*, p. 15.

8 Sanda Miller, *Constantin Brancusi: A Survey of his Work* (Oxford, 1995), pp. 7–9.

9 V. G. Paleolog, *Tineretea lui Brancusi* (Bucharest, 1967), pp. 21–2. Paleolog states that the house Brancusi was born in was built in the 1870s by his father; it was inherited by Brancusi's sister, who had it moved 200 metres and rebuilt on a new foundation. This rebuild is the Brancusi Museum today.

10 Petru Comarnescu, *Brancusi: Mit si metamorfoza in sculptura contemporana* (Bucharest, 1972), p. 26.

11 Paul Morand, *Brancusi*, exh. cat., Joseph Brummer Gallery, New York, 26 November–15 December (1926).

12 Sanda Miller, 'Reconfiguring Brancusi's Formative Years: Hobita – Craiova – Bucharest', in *Constantin Brancusi: The Essence of Things*, exh. cat., ed. Carmen Giménez and Matthew Gale, Tate Modern, London (2004), pp. 37–8.

13 Dinu C. Giurescu, 'Romania in epoca moderna', in *Istoria ilustrata a Romanilor* (Bucharest, 1981), pp. 318–526.

14 Paleolog, *Tineretea lui Brancusi*, pp. 17–19.

15 Ionel Jianou, *Constantin Brancusi* (London, 1963), p. 26.

16 Apriliana Medianu, 'In conversatie cu Brancusi', *Curentul* (6 October 1930), in Comarnescu, *Brancusi: Mit si metamorfoza in sculptura contemporana*, p. 48.

17 Vasile Blendea, nicknamed Trifu; oral communication to Romanian art historian Vasile Dragut in 1958, published in Barbu Brezianu, 'The Beginnings of Brancusi', *Art Journal*, xxv/1 (1965), pp. 15–25.

18 Miller, *Brancusi: A Survey*, p. 10.

19 Dan Smantanescu, 'Documente si amintiri despre Brancusi', *Arges* (March 1967), in Comarnescu, *Brancusi: Mit si metamorfoza in sculptura contemporana*, p. 69 and note 18.

2 Craiova and Apprenticeship

1 A. de Carlowitz, quoted in Nicolae Iorga, *Istoria Romanilor prin Calatori* (Bucharest, 1981), p. 551.

2 Sanda Miller, *Constantin Brancusi: A Survey of his Work* (Oxford, 1995), p. 41.

3 V. G. Paleolog, *Tineretea lui Brancusi* (Bucharest, 1967), p. 57.

4 Paul Rezeanu, 'Sculptorul Giorgio Vasilescu (1864–1898)' in *Historica i* (Bucharest, 1970), pp. 177–99.

5 Paul Rezeanu, 'Le sculpteur Constantin Bălăcescu (1865–1913)', in *Historica ii* (Bucharest, 1971), pp. 287–316.

6 Miller, *Brancusi: A Survey*, p. 11.

7 Miller, *Brancusi: A Survey*, p. 13.

8 Rezeanu, 'Le sculpteur Constantin Bălăcescu', p. 306.

9 Ion Biberi, 'De vorba cu Francisc Şirato', *Democratia*, 17 (June 1945). in *Artele Plastice in Oltenia (1821–1944)*, ed. P. Rezeanu (Craiova, 1980), p. 38.

10 Biberi, 'De vorba cu Francisc Şirato', pp. 39–40.

11 Petre Pandrea, *Portrete si controverse* (Bucharest, 1945), pp. 159–60.

12 Ionel Jianou, *Constantin Brancusi* (London, 1963), p. 24.

13 Paleolog, *Tineretea lui Brancusi*, p. 50.

14 Jianou, *Constantin Brancusi*, p. 24.

15 Sanda Miller, 'Reconfiguring Brancusi's Formative Years: Hobita – Craiova – Bucharest', in *Constantin Brancusi: The Essence of Things*, exh. cat., ed. Carmen Giménez and Matthew Gale, Tate Modern, London (2004), pp. 36–49.

16 *The Industrial Lyceum of Agricultural Mechanics, Craiova: 100 Years, 1871–1971* (Craiova, 1971).

17 Barbu Brezianu, *Brancusi in Romania* (Bucharest, 1976), pp. 199–204.

18 Petre Comarnescu, *Brancusi: Mit si metamorfoza in sculptura contemporana* (Bucharest, 1972), pp. 70–72.

19 Brezianu, *Brancusi in Romania*, p. 15.

20 The suggestion that Brancusi might have worked at the Thonet furniture factory in Vienna was made by Werner Hofmann , 'Discutii', in *Colocviul Brancusi, 13–15 October 1967* (Bucharest, 1968), pp. 152–5.

21 Paul Rezeanu, *Artele Plastice in Oltenia (1821–1944)* (Craiova, 1980), p. 62.

22 Brezianu, *Brancusi in Romania*, p. 206.

23 Ion Mocioi, *Constantin Brancusi – Viata* (Jassy, 2003), p. 38.

3 Bucharest and the Academy of Fine Arts

1 Sanda Miller, *Constantin Brancusi: A Survey of his Work* (Oxford, 1995), pp. 24–48.

2 Petre Pandrea, *Portrete si controverse* (Bucharest, 1945), p. 160.

3 Ion Mocioi, *Constantin Brancusi – Viata* (Jassy, 2003), p. 40.

4 Peter Neagoe, *The Saint of Montparnasse* (New York, 1965), p. 22.

5 Marie Bengesco, 'L'Art en Roumanie', in *La Roumanie en images* (Paris, 1919), pp. 26–7.

6 Bengesco, 'L'Art en Roumanie', p. 27.

7 Sanda Miller, 'Reconfiguring Brancusi's Formative Years: Hobita – Craiova – Bucharest', in *Constantin Brancusi: The Essence of Things*, exh. cat., ed. Carmen Giménez and Matthew Gale, Tate Modern, London (2004), pp. 42–3.

8 George Oprescu, 'Fundarea scolilor de arte frumoase, a pincotecilor si primele expozitii ale artisilor in viata', in *Pictura romaneasca in secolul XIX* (Bucharest, 1937).

9 Adrian-Silvan Ionescu, *Invatamantul artistic romanesc, 1830–1892* (Bucharest, 1999), pp. 120–21.

10 Albert Boime *The Academy and French Painting in the Nineteenth Century* (London, 1971), pp. 18–19.

11 Ionescu, *Invatamantul artistic romanesc*, pp. 159–72.

12 Ionescu, *Invatamantul artistic romanesc*, pp.163–6.

13 See Ion Hangiu, *Presa literara romaneasca* (Bucharest, 1968), 2 vols.

14 Miller, 'Reconfiguring Brancusi's Formative Years', pp. 46–7.

15 Alexandre Istrati and Natalia Dumitresco, *Brancusi* (Paris, 1986), p. 58.

16 Barbu Brezianu, *Brancusi in Romania* (Bucharest, 1976), pp. 158–92.

17 Discussed in Brezianu, *Brancusi in Romania*, pp. 158–92.

18 Antoine Etex, *Cours élémentaire de dessin* (Paris, 1877), quoted in Albert Boime, *The Academy and French Painting in the Nineteenth Century* (London, 1971), pp. 32–3.

19 Miller, *Brancusi: A Survey*, pp. 33–4.

20 Miller, *Brancusi: A Survey*, pp. 33–4.

21 Istrati and Dumitresco, *Brancusi*, illustrations 3, 4, 5, 6, 7, 8, 9, 10 and 11, pp. 272–4. Also Miller, *Brancusi: A Survey*, pp. 35–7.

22 Mocioi, *Brancusi – Viata*, pp. 56–7.

23 Sanda Miller, 'Paciurea's Chimeras', *Apollo* (October 2003), pp. 26–33.

24 Mocioi, *Brancusi – Viata*, p. 65.

25 Ionel Jianou, *Constantin Brancusi* (London, 1963), pp. 29–30.

4 Paris

1 Alexandre Istrati and Natalia Dumitresco, *Brancusi* (Paris, 1986), p. 62.

2 Ionel Jianou, *Constantin Brancusi* (London, 1963), p. 30.

3 Nigel Gosling, *Paris, 1900–1914* (London, 1978), p. 67.

4 Philippe Jullian, *Montmartre* (Oxford, 1977), pp. 32–9.

5 Roger Shattuck, *The Banquet Years: The Origins of the Avant-garde in France, 1885 to World War I* (New York, 1968), pp. 117–18.

6 John Richardson, *A Life of Picasso, volume I, 1881–1906* (London, 1992), p. 371.

7 Richardson, *A Life of Picasso, volume I*, p. 374.

8 Jean-Paul Crespelle, *La Vie quotidienne à Montparnasse à la Grande Epoque, 1905–1930* (Paris, 1976), pp. 12–13.

9 Crespelle, *La Vie quotidienne*, p. 32.

10 Crespelle, *La Vie quotidienne*, pp. 41–50.

11 Istrati and Dumitresco, *Brancusi*, pp. 65–8.

12 Petre Pandrea, *Portrete si controverse* (Bucharest, 1945), p. 160.

13 Istrati and Dumitresco, *Brancusi*, p. 65.

14 Sanda Miller, *Constantin Brancusi: A Survey of his Work* (Oxford, 1995), pp. 49–62.

15 Doina Lemny, 'Les Archives', in *La Dation Brancusi (dessins et archives)*, exh. cat., Centre Georges Pompidou, Paris (2003), p. 207 note 4.

16 Petre Comarnescu, *Mit si metammorfoza in sculptura contemporana* (Bucharest, 1972), p. 119.

17 Petre Pandrea, *Portrete si controverse*, p. 160.

18 Barbu Brezianu, *Brancusi in Romania* (Bucharest, 1976), p. 100.

19 Miller, *Brancusi: A Survey*, pp. 67–8.

20 Marielle Tabart and Isabel Monod-Fontaine, *Brancusi photographe*, exh. cat., Musée National d'Art Moderne, Centre National d'Art et de Culture, Paris (1973), p. 14, fig. 2: 'Vue d'atelier à la prière, 54, rue du Montparnasse, vers 1907'.

21 Istrati and Dumitresco, *Brancusi*, p. 73.

22 Tabart and Monod-Fontaine, *Brancusi photographe*, no. 2: 'Vue d'atelier à La prière, 54, rue du Montparnasse,vers 1907, and no. 5: 'Vue d'atelier avec modèle, fin 1907, p. 117.

23 Peter Neagoe, *The Saint of Montparnasse* (New York, 1963), p. 8.

24 Istrati and Dumitresco, *Brancusi*, pp. 73–4.

25 Brezianu, *Brancusi in Romania*, pp. 230–31.

26 Brezianu, *Brancusi in Romania*, pp. 230–31.

27 Frederich Teja-Bach, Margit Rowell and Ann Temkin, *Constantin Brancusi, 1876–1957*, exh. cat., Musée National d'Art Moderne, Paris (1995), pp. 102–5, 164–5, 198–9.

28 Philippe Thiébaut, *Picasso oeuvres reçues en paiement des droits de succession* (Paris, 1979), p. 50.

29 John Richardson, *A Life of Picasso, volume II: 1907–1917* (New York, 1996), p. 43.

30 Doina Lemny, *Constantin Brancusi* (Jassy, 2005), p. 56.

31 V. G. Paleolog, 'Brancusi, Brancusi II', the MS of 1976, pp. 110–14 (translation by Sanda Miller).

32 Paleolog, 'Brancusi, Brancusi II', pp. 110–14.

33 The two letters in the collection of MoMA, New York, were first published by Sidney Geist in *Brancusi: A Study of the Sculpture by Sidney Geist* (London, 1968), Appendix no. 11, pp. 190–92.

34 *A Study of the Sculpture*, pp. 190–92.

35 *A Study of the Sculpture*, pp. 190–92.

36 Miller, *Brancusi: A Survey*, p. 135.

37 Miller, *Brancusi: A Survey*, pp. 137–8.

38 Lemny, *Constantin Brancusi*, pp. 56–7.

39 Istrati and Dumitresco, *Brancusi* (fig. 60), *Brancusi, La Muse endormie I* (1908), marble, p. 283 (fig. 70); *Une Muse* (1912), marble, p. 286 (fig. 73); *Mlle Pogany I* (1912), plaster, p. 286 (fig. 74); *Torse de jeune fille* (1913), p. 286 (fig. 60); *Le Baiser* (1912), stone, p. 286.

40 Frank Crowninshield, 'The Scandalous Armory Show of 1913', *Vogue* (September 1940), in *The Armory Show Anthology* (New York, 1972), pp. 69–116.

41 Istrati and Dumitresco, *Brancusi*, p. 130.

42 Pandrea, *Portrete si controverse*, p. 169.

43 Istrati and Dumitresco, *Brancusi*, pp. 131–2.

44 Nina Hamnett, *Laughing Torso* (London, 1932), p. 123.

45 Teja-Bach, Rowell and Temkin, *Brancusi, 1876–1957*, p. 138.

46 Marielle Tabart, 'Les Avatars de la "Princesse X"', in *Les Carnets de l'Atelier Brancusi*, La série et l'oeuvre unique, Centre National d'Art et de Culture, Georges Pompidou, Paris (1999), pp. 8–13.

47 Sanda Miller, 'Brancusi's Women', *Apollo* (March 2007), pp. 56–63.

48 Miller, *Brancusi: A Survey*, pp. 103–4.

49 Athena T. Spear, 'A Contribution to Brancusi Chronology', *Art Bulletin*, 48 (March 1966), pp. 45–9.

50 Barbu Brezianu, 'Le Secret du Baiser de Brancusi', *La Revue du Louvre*, I (1969), pp. 25–30.

51 Daniel-Henri Kahnweiler, 'L'Art nègre et le cubisme', *Presence Africaine*, 3 (1948), p. 267, reprinted in *Confessions esthetiques* (Paris, 1963).

52 Jean Laude, *La Peinture française (1905–1914) et 'l'art nègre' (Contribution à l'étude des sources du fauvisme et du cubisme)* (Paris, 1968), pp. 102–3.

53 Istrati and Dumitresco, *Brancusi*, fig. 47: *La Sagesse de la terre*, p. 281.

54 Brezianu, *Brancusi in Romania*, pp. 115–17.

55 Miller, *Brancusi: A Survey*, pp. 72–7.

56 Athena Tacha-Spear, *Brancusi's Birds* (New York, 1969).

57 Istrati and Dumitresco, *Brancusi*, pp. 284–6: 1 *Măiastra*, white marble, 1910, fig. 64; p. 284, 2 *Măiastra*, polished bronze, 1911, fig.65; p. 285, 3 *Măiastra*, 1911, gilded bronze, fig. 68; p. 285, 4 *Măiastra*, 1912, polished bronze, fig. 72, p. 286; 5 *Măiastra*, polished bronze, 1912, (no illustration) p. 286.

58 Sanda Miller, 'In illo tempore: Măiastra', *Les Carnets de l'atelier Brancusi: La série et l'oeuvre unique*, Centre National d'Art et de Culture, Georges Pompidou, Paris (2001), pp. 13–20.

59 Carola Giedion-Welcker, *Contemporary Sculpture: An Evolution in Volume and Space* (revd edn, London, 1961), p. 138.

60 Jianou, *Constantin Brancusi*, p. 37.

61 Pandrea, *Portrete si controverse*, p. 160.

62 Guillaume Apollinaire: 'The Russian Painters in the Impasse Ronsin – the Truth About the Steinheil Case', *L'Intransigent* (31 October 1910), in *Apollinaire on Art: Essays and Reviews, 1902–1918*, Documents of 20th Century Art (London, 1972), pp. 115–16.

63 'The Russian Painters in the Impasse Ronsin', pp. 115–16.

64 'The Russian Painters in the Impasse Ronsin', pp. 115–16.

65 Athena Tacha-Spear, 'Elie Nadelman's Early Heads (1905–1911)', *Allen Memorial Art Museum Bulletin*, xviii/3 (Spring 1971), p. 208.

66 Lincoln Kirstein, *The Sculpture of Elie Nadelman* (New York, 1948), p. 18.

67 Tacha-Spear, 'Nadelman's Early Heads', p. 206.

68 Kirstein, *Nadelman*, pp. 11–12 and note 70.

69 Richardson, *A Life of Picasso, volume ii*, p. 146.

70 Alfred Werner, *Modigliani the Sculptor* (London, 1965), p. 25.

71 Quoted in Werner, *Modigliani the Sculptor*, p. 21.

72 Quoted in Werner, *Modigliani the Sculptor*, p. 22.

73 Jeanne Modigliani, 'Modigliani sans Légende', in *Amedeo Modigliani, 1884–1920*, exh. cat., Musée d'Art de la Ville de Paris (1981), p. 79.

74 Carol Mann, *Modigliani* (London, 1980), p. 58.

75 Jacob Epstein, *An Autobiography* (London, 1964), pp. 46–7.

76 Miller, *Brancusi: A Survey*, pp. 123–30 and note 78.

77 Miller, *Brancusi: A Survey*, p. 130.

78 André Gide, *The Journals* (New York, 1947), vol. I, pp. 234–7; quoted in Kirstein, *Nadelman*, p. 18.

79 Miller, *Brancusi: A Survey*, p. 175.

5 The Studios at impasse Ronsin

1 Alexandre Istrati and Natalia Dumitresco, *Brancusi* (Paris, 1986), p. 1.

2 Marielle Tabart, 'Histoire et fonction de l'atelier', in *La Collection l'Atelier Brancusi*, Centre Georges Pompidou, Paris (1997), pp. 26–7.

3 Sanda Miller, *Constantin Brancusi: A Survey of his Work* (Oxford, 1995), p. 178.

4 Miller, *Brancusi: A Survey*, pp. 178–83.

5 Miller, *Brancusi: A Survey*, p. 188.

6 Istrati and Dumitresco, *Brancusi*, p. 92.

7 Doina Lemny, 'Maurice et Morice: chronique d'une amitie', in *Brancusi et Duchamp*, exh. cat., Centre National d'Art et de Culture, Georges Pompidou, Paris (2000), pp. 21–2.

8 The testimony of Lydie Levassor (Marcel Duchamp's first wife), in Istrati and Dumitresco, *Brancusi*, p. 267 note 6.

9 Marielle Tabart and Isabelle Monod-Fontaine, *Brancusi photographe* (Paris, 1979).

10 Sanda Miller, 'Constantin Brancusi's Photographs', *Artforum* (March 1981), pp. 38–44.

11 Man Ray, *Self-Portrait* (New York, 1979), p. 211.

12 Istrati and Dumitresco, *Brancusi*, pp. 94–5.

13 Jacob Epstein, *An Autobiography* (London, 1964), pp. 131–5.

14 Man Ray, *Self-Portrait*, pp. 208–9.

15 Sanda Miller, *Brancusi: A Survey*, pp. 178–83.

16 Barbu Brezianu, 'Pages inédites de la correspondance de Brancusi', *Revue Roumaine d'Histoire de l'Art*, 2 (1964), pp. 385–400.

17 Tabart and Monod-Fontaine, *Brancusi photographe*, no. 25: 'Fernand Léger dans l'atelier', vers 1922; no. 48: 'Man Ray dans l'atelier', vers 1930; and no. 49: 'Brancusi et une de ses amies' vers 1930 (unpaginated).

18 Cited in Petru Comarnescu, *Mit si metamorfoza in sculptura contemporana* (Bucharest, 1972), p. 116.

19 Epstein, *Autobiography*, p. 48.

20 André Salmon, *Souvenirs sans fin (Première époque: 1903–1908)* (Paris, 1955), p. 170.

21 Fernande Olivier, *Picasso and his Friends* (New York, 1965); quoted in John Richardson: *A Life of Picasso, volume I: 1881–1906* (London, 1991), p. 309.

22 John Richardson: *A Life of Picasso, volume II: 1907–1917* (New York, 1996), p. 34.

23 Istrati and Dumitresco, *Brancusi*, p. 103.

24 Marielle Tabart, 'L'Atelier comme lieu de presentation et d'exposition', *La Collection l'Atelier Brancusi*, exh. cat., Centre Georges Pompidou, Paris (1997), pp. 38–52.

25 Jeanne Robert Foster: 'Constantin Brancusi: A Note on the Man and the Formal Perfection of his Carvings', *Vanity Fair* (May 1922), pp. 6–8.

26 Nina Hamnett, *Laughing Torso* (London, 1932), pp. 123–4.

27 Dorothy Adlow, 'Brancusi', *Drawing and Design*, vol. II (London, 1927), pp. 37–41.

28 Peggy Guggenheim in Christian Zervos, *Constantin Brancusi (sculptures, peintures, fresques, dessins)* (Paris, 1957), p. 88.

29 Carola Giedion-Welcker, *Constantin Brancusi* (Neuchâtel, 1959).

30 Carola Giedion-Welcker in Zervos, *Constantin Brancusi*, p. 88.

31 Peggy Guggenheim in Zervos, *Constantin Brancusi*, pp. 88–9.

32 Peggy Guggenheim, *Out of this Century (Confessions of an Art Addict)* (London, 1980), pp. 211–12.

33 Bohdan Urbanowicz, 'Vizita mea la Brancusi, decembrie 1956', *Colocviul Brancusi*, Bucharest, 13–15 October 1967 (Bucharest, 1968), pp. 108–9.

34 Urbanowicz, 'Vizita mea la Brancusi', p. 109.

6 Work and Friends

1 Jean Arp, 'La Dolonne sans fin', in Cristian Zervos, *Constantin Brancusi (sculptures, peintures, fresques, dessins)* (Paris, 1957), p. 30.

2 Ionel Jianou, *Constantin Brancusi* (London, 1963), p. 41.

3 Doina Lemny, 'Les Archives', *La Dation Brancusi (dessins et archives)*, exh. cat., Centre Georges Pompidou, Paris (2003), pp. 105–15.

4 Alexandre Istrati and Natalia Dumitresco, *Brancusi* (Paris, 1986), 'Vue de la salle d'exposition de l'Armory Show avec l'envoi de Brancusi', p. 90.

5 Lemny, 'Les Archives', p. 203.

6 Lemny, 'Les Archives', p. 106.

7 Lemny, 'Les Archives', p. 107.

8 The New York Public Library has 36 letters and telegrams, dated between 4 October 1916 (letter from Brancusi to Walter Pach) to 16 February 1923 (letter from John Quinn to Brancusi). Thirty letters and telegrams dated between 19 January 1917 (Brancusi to Quinn) and 17 December 1923 (Brancusi to Quinn), some of which are the same letters as the ones in the NYPL, have been published in Doina Lemny, 'Les Archives', pp. 135–54.

9 Lemny, 'Les Archives', pp. 135–55.

10 B. L. Reid, *John Quinn and his Friends* (Oxford, 1968), p. 652.

11 Forbes Watson, *John Quinn (1870–1925): Collection of Paintings, Water Colours, Drawings and Sculpture* (New York, 1926).

12 Ian Mackillop, *Free Spirits* (London, 2001), p. 142.

13 Mackillop, *Free Spirits*, pp. 143–4.

14 Lemny, 'Les Archives', pp. 155–66.

15 Lemny, 'Les Archives', p. 155.

16 Lemny, 'Les Archives', p. 166.

17 Petre Pandrea, *Portrete si controverse* (Bucharest, 1945), pp. 161–2.

18 Mary E. Davis, *Erik Satie* (London, 2007), pp. 122–3.

19 V. G. Paleolog, *Despre Satie si noul muzicalism* (Bucharest, 1945), p. 47.

20 Paleolog, *Despre Satie si noul muzicalism*, p. 15.

21 Pandrea, *Portrete si controverse*, p. 170.

22 Irina Codreanu, 'Ucenicie la Brancusi', *Colocviul Brancusi, Bucharest 13–15 October 1967* (Bucharest, 1968), pp. 57–8.

23 Codreanu, 'Ucenicie la Brancusi', p. 58.

24 Istrati and Dumitresco, *Brancusi*, p. 145.

25 Sanda Miller, *Constantin Brancusi: A Survey of his Work* (Oxford, 1995), p. 184.

26 Hans Richter, *Dada: Art and Anti-Art* (London, 1978), p. 181.

27 Istrati and Dumitresco, *Brancusi*, pp. 135–6.

28 Richter, *Dada*, pp. 18–19.

29 Istrati and Dumitresco, *Brancusi*, p. 142.

30 Barbu Brezianu, *Brancusi in Romania* (Bucharest, 1978), fig. 70 (p. 245), *Snail and Birds*, 1929, and fig. 71 (p. 245), *Horned Animal*, 1929. Both these drawings were exhibited in Bucharest at the Salon of Drawings

and Prints in 1929. A third abstract drawing is not reproduced here.

31 Benjamin Fondane, 'Brancusi', *Cahiers de l'étoile* (September–October 1929), pp. 708–25.

32 Paul Daniel, 'Destinul unui poet', in *Beniamin Fundoianu: Poezii* (Bucharest, 1978), pp. 595–642.

33 Mihai Mihailovici, 'Recollections', in Jianou, *Constantin Brancusi*, p. 50.

34 V. G. Paleolog, *Tineretea lui Brancusi* (Bucharest, 1967), p. 82.

35 Jean-Paul Crespelle, *La Vie quotidienne à Montparnasse à la Grande Epoque, 1905–1930* (Paris, 1976), pp. 132–3.

36 Nina Hamnett, *Laughing Torso* (London, 1932), p. 195.

37 Istrati and Dumitresco, *Brancusi*, p. 146.

38 Lemny, 'Les Archives', p. 177.

39 1910 Salon, Grand Palais Champs-Elysées, *Catalogue des oeuvres exposées*: *Margit Pogany*, no. 960; *Nature Morte*, no. 961; *Femme lisant*, p. 153.

40 Doina Lemny, *Constantin Brancusi* (Jassy, 2005), pp. 203–19.

41 V. G. Paleolog, 'Brancusi, Brancusi II' (the unpublished MS completed in 1976), p. 120.

42 Istrati and Dumitresco, *Brancusi*, pp. 147–8.

43 Istrati and Dumitresco, *Brancusi*, p. 146.

44 Barbu Brezianu, 'Les Débuts de Brancusi', *Revue Roumaine d'Histoire de l'Art*, I/2 (1964), pp. 85–loo.

45 Sanda Miller, 'Brancusi's Women', *Apollo* (March 2006), p. 59.

46 Lemny, 'Les Amis', *La Dation Brancusi*, pp. 213–15.

47 Lemny, 'Les Amis', pp. 218–21.

48 Lemny, 'Les Amis', pp. 215–18.

49 Istrati and Dumitresco, *Brancusi*, fig. 21 (p. 276): *Mme Victoria Vaschide*.

50 Miller, 'Brancusi's Women', pp. 59–63.

51 Miller, 'Brancusi's Women', pp. 59–60.

52 *This Quarter* (Art Supplement), I/1 [Paris] (1925), pp. 235–7.

53 Roger Shattuck, *The Banquet Years: The Origins of the Avant-Garde in France, 1885 to World War I* (New York, 1968), p. 161.

54 Miller, *Brancusi: A Survey*, pp. 195–6.

55 Arthur Miller, *Einstein, Picasso: Space, Time and the Beauty that Causes Havoc* (London, 2002).

56 Marielle Tabart, 'Inventory of Brancusi's personal library, 1960'. Brancusi archives, Centre National d'Art et de Culture, Georges Pompidou, Paris.

57 Carola Giedion-Welcker, *Contemporary Sculpture (An Evolution in Volume and Space)* (London, 1960), p. 140.

58 Plato, *The Symposium*, trans. Walter Hamilton (Harmondsworth, 1951), p. 95.

59 Ionel Jianou, 'Tradition et universalité dans l'art de Brancusi', in Petru Comarnescu, Mircea Eliade, Ionel Jianou and Constantin Noica, *Brancusi: Introduction, Témoignages* (Paris, 1982), p. 141.

7 Tîrgu-Jiu

1 Alexandre Istrati and Natalia Dumitresco, *Brancusi* (Paris, 1986), p. 212.

2 Barbu Brezianu, 'Pages inédites de la correspondance de Brancusi', *Revue Roumaine d'Histoire de l'Art*, 1/1 (1964), pp. 385–400.

3 Stefan Geogescu-Gorjan, 'The Column Without End', *Revue Roumaine d'Histoire de l'Art*, 1/1 (1964), pp. 279–93.

4 Geogescu-Gorjan, 'The Column Without End', pp. 279–93.

5 Carola Giedion-Welcker, 'Coloana fara sfirsit a lui Constantin Brancusi', *Secolul*, xx/10–12 (1976), p. 217.

6 Sanda Miller, *Constantin Brancusi: A Survey of his Work* (Oxford, 1995), pp. 205–6.

7 Man Ray, *Self-Portrait* (New York, 1979), pp. 212–13.

8 Georgescu-Gorjan, 'The Column Without End', pp. 279–93.

9 Georgescu-Gorjan, 'The Column Without End', pp. 287–8.

10 Georgescu-Gorjan, 'The Column Without End', pp. 290–92.

11 Interview (Bucharest 10 May 1978) with Sanda Tătărăscu, the daughter of Arethie Tătărăscu, who was 11 years of age when Brancusi was invited to Tîrgu-Jiu.

12 Ion Mocioi, *Constantin Brancusi – Viata* (Jassy, 2003), p. 304.

13 Mocioi, *Constantin Brancusi – Viata*, p. 310.

14 Ionel Jianou, 'L'Ensemble monumental de Tîrgu-Jiu', in Petru Comarnescu, Mircea Eliade, Ionel Jianou and Constantin Noica, *Brancusi, Introduction, Témoignages* (Paris, 1982), p. 54.

15 Ion Alexandrescu, 'Amintire despre Brancusi', in Ion Mocioi, ed., *Marturii despre Bancusi* (Tîrgu-Jiu, 1975), pp. 36–45.

16 V. G. Paleolog, *Constantin Brancusi* (Bucharest, 1947), p. 46.

17 Ionel Jianou, *Constantin Brancusi* (London, 1963), p. 58.

18 Ion Alexandrescu, 'Amintire despre Brancusi', pp. 36–45.

19 Ibid., pp. 40–41.

20 Ibid., p. 43.

21 These details were communicated to Ionel Jianou by V. G. Paleolog and his son, Tretie Paleolog (also a Brancusi scholar): Jianou, 'L'Ensemble monumental de Tîrgu-Jiu', p. 55.

22 Jianou *Constantin Brancusi*, p. 57.

23 Flora Merrill, 'Brancusi the Sculptor of the Spirit, Would Build "Infinite Column" in Park', *New York World* (3 October 1926).

24 Camilla Grey, *The Russian Experiment in Art, 1863–1922* (London, 1976), pp. 225–6.

25 Istrati and Dumitresco, *Brancusi*, pp. 256–9.

26 Communicated to Jianou by Paleolog and his son: Jianou, 'L'Ensemble monumental de Tîrgu-Jiu', pp. 55–6.

27 Jianou, *Constantin Brancusi*, p. 55.

28 V. G. Paleolog, *Constantin Brancusi* (Bucharest, 1947), p. 46.

29 Mocioi, *Constantin Brancusi – Viata*, pp. 350–53. For these quotations see *Finnegans Wake*, p. 5 (all English-language editions are paginated identically).

30 Istrati and Dumitresco, *Brancusi*, p. 216.

8 Last Works, Last Friends, Legacy

1 David Lewis, *Brancusi* (London, 1957), p. 5.

2 Carola Giedion-Welcker, *Constantin Brancusi* (Neuchâtel, 1959), p. 198.

3 William Carlos Williams, 'Brancusi', *Magazine of Art* [New York] (December 1955), cited in Ionel Jianou, *Constantin Brancusi* (London, 1963), p. 59.

4 Clement Greenberg, 'The Situation at the Moment', *Partisan Review* (January 1948), quoted in Guillbaut, *How New York Stole the Idea of Modern Art: Abstract Expressionism, Freedom and the Cold War* (Chicago, 1983), p. 16.

5 Bernard Ceysson, 'A Propos des années cinquante : tradition et modernite', in *Vingt-cinq ans d'art en France*, ed. Bernard Ceysson et al. (Paris, 1986), p. 17.

6 Ceysson, 'A Propos des années cinquante', pp. 16–18.

7 Max Kozloff, 'American Painting During the Cold War', *Artforum*, no. 9 (May 1973), pp. 43–54, and Eva Cockroft, 'Abstract Expressionism: Weapon of the Cold War', *Artforum*, no. 10 (June 1974), pp. 39–41, in Francusi Francina, ed., *Pollock and After* (London, 1985), pp. 107–24 and 115–34.

8 Maurice de Vlaminck, 'Mon Testament (j'air fait ce que j'ai pu, j'ai peint ce que j'ai vu)', *Arts-Spectacles* (2–8 January 1957), p. 1 (Archives of CNAC, Centre Georges Pompidou, Paris).

9 Doina Lemny, *Constantin Brancusi* (Jassy, 2005), pp. 239–41.

10 Dora Valier, 'Vendredi 4 Mai, 1956 chez Brancusi', in Christian Zervos, *Constantin Brancusi (sculptures, peintures, fresques, dessins)* (Paris, 1957), pp. 24–8.

11 Valentine Hugo in Zervos, *Constantin Brancusi*, pp. 100–2.

12 Alexandre Istrati and Natalia Dumitresco, *Brancusi* (Paris, 1986), pp. 258–9.

13 Ionel Jianou, *Constantin Brancusi* (London, 1963), p. 61.

14 *La Dation Brancusi (dessins et archives)*, the catalogue of an exhibition held at CNAC, Centre Georges Pompidou, Paris, 25 June–15 September 2003, ed. Doina Lemny and Marielle Tabart. (Doina Lemny has since published a book in Romanian on the archives: *Constantin Brancusi*, Jassy, 2005.)

When Brancusi died in 1957 he nominated two Romanian painters, Alexandre Istrati and Natalia Dumitreso (Dumitreso arrived in Paris in 1947 from Bucharest on a scholarship to study painting, and took lodgings with Brancusi), as his legatees. Only a small part of the archives, however, was available to researchers even after the publication in 1986 of Istrati and Dumitresco's book on Brancusi, prefaced by Pontus Hulten, the then director of MNAM, Centre Georges Pompidou. Istrati and Dumitresco's heirs have recently donated the rest of the archives, now known as *La Dation Brancusi 2001*, to the Centre National d'Art et de Culture (CNAC) Georges Pompidou, Paris, at a time when the bulk of Brancusi's private correspondence became available for the first time to scholars. *La Dation Brancusi 2001* contains 97 drawings and *circa* 6,000 sheets of material hitherto inaccessible to scholars.

Select Bibliography

Adlow, Dorothy, 'Constantin Brancusi', *Drawing and Design*, II (1927)

Apollinaire, Guillaume, *Apollinaire on Art: Essays and Reviews, 1902–1918*, Documents of Twentieth Century Art (London, 1972)

Bengesco, Marie, 'L'Art en Roumanie', in *La Roumanie en images* (Paris, 1919)

Brancusi, Constantin, 'Aphorismes', *This Quarter*, Art Supplement (1925), pp. 236–7

Brezianu, Barbu, 'The Beginnings of Brancusi', *Art Journal*, XXV/1 (1965), pp. 15–25

——, *Brancusi in Romania* (Bucharest, 1976)

——, 'Pages inédites de la correspondance de Brancusi', *Revue Roumaine d'Histoire de l'Art*, 1/1 (1964), pp. 385–400

——, 'Le Secret du Baiser de Brancusi', *La Revue du Louvre*, 1 (1969), pp. 25–30

Comarnescu, Petre, *Mit si metamorfoza in sculptura contemporana* (Bucharest, 1972)

——, Mircea Eliade, Ionel Jianou and Constantin Noica, *Brancusi, Introduction, Témoignages* (Paris, 1982)

Crespelle, Jean-Pierre, *La Vie quotidienne a Montparnasse a la grande époque: 1905–1930* (Paris, 1976)

——, *La Vie quotidienne à Montmartre au temps de Picasso, 1900–1930* (Paris, 1978)

Epstein, Jacob, *An Autobiography* (London, 1964)

Foster, Jeanne Robert, 'Constantin Brancusi: A Note on the Man and the Formal Perfection of his Carvings', *Vanity Fair* (May 1922), pp. 6–8

Geist, Sidney, *Brancusi: A Study of the Sculpture* (London, 1968)

Georgescu-Gorjan, Stefan, 'Coloanele infinite ale lui Brancusi' (Arhiva Brancusi), *Arta*, 8 (1977), pp. 19–21

——, 'The Genesis of the Column without End', *Revue Roumaine d'Histoire de l'Art*, 1 and 2 (1964), pp. 279–93

Giedion-Welcker, Carola, *Constantin Brancusi* (Neuchâtel, 1959)

——, *Contemporary Sculpture: An Evolution in Volume and Space*, revd edn (London, 1961)

Gosling, Nigel, *Paris 1900–1914: The Miraculous Years* (London, 1978)

Green, Christopher, *Art in France, 1900–1940* (New Haven, CT, and London, 2000)

Hamnett, Nina, *Laughing Torso* (London, 1932)

Hoffman, Malvina, *Sculpture Inside and Out* (New York, 1939)

Ionescu, Adrian-Silvan, *Invatamantul artistic romanesc, 1830–1892* (Bucharest, 1999)

Istrati, Alexandre and Natalia Dumitresco, *Brancusi* (Paris, 1986)

Jianou, Ionel, *Constantin Brancusi* (London, 1963)

Jullian, Philippe, *Montmartre* (Oxford, 1977)

Kahnweiler, Daniel-Henri, 'L'Art negre et le cubisme', *Présence africaine*, 3 (1948), pp. 367–78

——, *Confessions esthétiques* (Paris, 1963)

Kallestrup, Shona, *Art and Design in Romania, 1866–1927* (New York, 2006)

Kirstein, Lincoln, *Elie Nadelman* (New York, 1973)

——, *The Sculpture of Elie Nadelman* (New York, 1948)

Laude, Jean, *La Peinture française (1905–1914) et 'l'art nègre' (Contribution à l'étude des sources du fauvisme et du cubisme)* (Paris, 1968)

Lemny, Doina, 'Maurice et Morice: chronique d'une amitie', *Brancusi et Duchamp,*

Les Carnets de l'atelier Brancusi, Regards Historiques Brancusi et Duchamp (Paris, 2000)

——, *Constantin Brancusi* (Jassy, 2005)

Lewis, David, *Brancusi* (London, 1957)

Machedon, Luminita, and Ernie Schoffham, *Romanian Modernism: The Architecture of Bucharest, 1920–1940* (Cambridge, MA, 1999)

Man Ray, *Self-Portrait Man Ray* (New York, 1963)

Mann, Carol, *Modigliani* (London, 1980)

Merrill, Flora, 'Brancusi, the Sculptor of the Spirit, would Build "Infinite Column" in Park', *New York World* (3 October, 1926)

Miller, Arthur, *Einstein, Picasso: Space, Time and the Beauty that Causes Havoc* (London, 2002)

Miller, Sanda, 'Constantin Brancusi's Photographs', *Artforum* (March 1981),
     pp. 38–44

——, *Constantin Brancusi: A Survey of his Work* (Oxford, 1995)

——, 'In illo tempore, Măiastra', *Les Carnets de l'Atelier Brancusi; La Série
     et l'oeuvre unique* (Paris, 2001), pp. 13–20

——, 'Paciurea's Chimeras', *Apollo* (October 2003), pp. 26–33

——, 'Reconfiguring Brancusi's Formative Years: Hobita – Craiova –
     Bucharest', in *Constantin Brancusi: The Essence of Things*, ed. Carmen
     Giménez and Matthew Gale (London, 2004), pp. 36–49

——, 'Brancusi's Women', *Apollo* (March 2006), pp. 59–63

Mocioi, Ion, *Constantin Brancusi – Viata* (Jassy, 2003)

Neagoe, Peter, *The Saint of Montparnasse* (New York, 1965)

Oprescu, George, *Peasant Art in Romania* (London, 1929)

——, *Pictura Romaneasca in secolul XIX, Biblioteca artistic, Fundatia pentru
     literature si arta Regele Carol II* (Bucharest, 1937)

——, *Sculptura Romaneasca* (Bucharest, 1965)

Paleolog, V. G., *Brancusi: Brancusi I* (Craiova, 1976)

——, 'Brancusi, Brancusi II', MS. 1976

——, *Despre Eric Satie si noul muzicalism* (Bucharest, 1945)

——, *Tineretea lui Brancusi* (Bucharest, 1967)

Pandrea, Petre, *Portrete si controverse* (Bucharest, 1945)

Reid, B. L, *The Man from New York: John Quinn and his Friends* (New York, 1968)

Rezeanu, Paul, 'Le sculpteur Constantin Balacescu (1865–1913), *Historica II*,
     Academia de Stiinte Sociale si Politice a Republicii Socialiste Romania
     (Bucharest, 1971)

——, 'Sculptorul Giorgio Vasilescu (1864–1898), *Historica I*, Academia de
     Stiinte Sociale si Politice a Republicii Socialiste Romania (Bucharest,
     1970)

——, *Artele Plastice in Oltenia (1821–1944)* (Craiova, 1980)

Richardson, John, *A Life of Picasso, volume I: 1881–1906* (London, 1992);
     volume II: 1907–1917 (New York, 1996)

Richter, Hans, *Dada: Art and Anti-Art* (London, 1965)

Shattuck, Roger, *The Banquet Years: The Origins of the Avant-Garde in France,
     1885 to World War I* (New York, 1968)

Spear, Athena Tacha, *Brancusi's Birds* (New York, 1969)

Tabart Marielle and Isabelle Monod-Fontaine, *Brancusi photographe* (Paris,
     1977)

Tabart Marielle, 'Histoire et fonction de l'atelier', in *La Collection l'Atelier Brancusi* (Paris, 1997), pp. 26–7

——, 'L'Atelier comme lieu de mémoire', in *La Collection l'Atelier Brancusi* (Paris, 1997), pp. 68–182

——, and Doina Lemny, *La Dation Brancusi (dessins and archives)*, exh. cat., Centre National d'Art et de Culture, Georges Pompidou, 25 June–15 Sept 2003 (Paris, 2003)

Werner, Alfred, *Modigliani the Sculptor* (London, 1965)

Zervos, Christian, ed., *Constantin Brancusi (sculptures, peintures, fresques, dessins)* (Paris, 1957)

Acknowledgements

My interest in Constantin Brancusi stretches back to the 1970s, when I embarked on a PhD at the Courtauld Institute of Art in London. I was born in Romania, and in my research my knowledge of the language and culture enabled me to bridge the gap between Romanian and West European scholarship. During this period I was helped, supported and encouraged by many people, but I would like to mention two friends in particular: Marielle Tabart, former curator of the Atelier Brancusi, and one of the leading Brancusi scholars, has been an invaluable help; and so, more recently, has Doina Lemny, curator at CNAC, Centre Georges Pompidou, Paris. I benefited from the material made available to Brancusi scholars in 2001 when *La Dation Brancusi 2001* became public; and in particular with the exhibition in 2003 of this final part of the Brancusi archives, hitherto in private hands but now in the possession of CNAC, Paris. The exhibition was accompanied by an excellent catalogue, *La Dation Brancusi*, researched and written by Marielle and Doina. Material in the French archive has been invaluable for this book.

I wish to thank my collaborator and friend of many years, Mihai Oroveanu, himself an accomplished photographer, who supplied the visual material for this book, including historical and rare images of nineteenth-century Romania, from his vast personal collection of photographs.

I would also like to thank Vivian Constantinopoulos at Reaktion; without her interest and keeness to add the name of Brancusi to the distinguished roll call of names of intellectuals and artists featured in the Critical Lives series, this book would not have been written. Warm thanks as well to Robert Williams for his editorial input.

The generous financial support of Southampton Solent University made possible the inclusion of visual material in this book. I would like to express my gratitude in particular to our Dean of Faculty of Media, Arts & Society, Professor Rod Pilling, and my colleague and friend Suzanne Dixon, Head of the School of Communication and Media, whose invaluable and continuous support is appreciated.

Finally, my thanks to my daughter Giulia for her love and support; this book is dedicated to her.

Photo Acknowledgements

The author and publishers wish to express their thanks to the following sources of illustrative material and/or permission to reproduce it (some locations of artworks are also given below):

© ADAGP, Paris, and DACS, London, 2010: pp. 38, 49, 50, 52, 53, 57, 59, 66, 82, 95, 112, 122, 131, 132, 133, 149; Brancusi photographic archive, Centre National d'Art Contemporain, Paris: pp. 6, 38, 45, 49, 50, 52, 78, 82, 87, 88, 95, 112, 120, 122, 128, 142; Centre National d'Art Contemporain, Paris: p. 59; photo Vivian Constantinopoulos: p. 149; Hirshhorn Museum and Sculpture Garden, Smithsonian Institution, Washington, DC: p. 53; photo © LL/Roger-Viollet, courtesy of Rex Features: p. 41; Musée National d'Art Moderne, Paris: p. 73; The Museum of Modern Art, New York: p. 57; photos Mihai Oroveanu: pp. 15, 16, 131, 132, 133; Mihai Oroveanu collection, Bucharest: pp. 14, 15, 16, 22, 25, 26, 31, 35, 36, 85, 89, 131, 132, 133; Philadelphia Museum of Art: p. 66; present location unknown: p. 52; photo © Roger-Viollet, courtesy Rex Features: p. 32; photo © Jean-Régis Roustan/Roger-Viollet, courtesy Rex Features: p. 79; after Marielle Tabart, *La Collection l'atelier Brancusi* (Paris, 1997): p. 77.

Printed and bound by CPI Group (UK) Ltd, Croydon, CR0 4YY

23/06/2026

14906073-0001